MONEY QUEENS

The author would like to acknowledge the Gadigal people of the Eora Nation, who are the Traditional Custodians of the land on which this book was written. I pay my respects to Elders past, present and emerging and acknowledge that sovereignty was never ceded.

Published by Affirm Press, 2022

Boon Wurrung Country
28 Thistlethwaite Street
South Melbourne, VIC 3205

1 3 5 7 9 10 8 6 4 2

ISBN: 9781922711946 (paperback)

Printed and bound in China by RR Donnelley Printing Solutions Ltd

MONEY QUEENS

RULE your MONEY

Disclaimer

The information in this book is of a general nature only and does not represent professional advice. It does not take into account your financial situation, objectives or needs. Before acting on any of this information, you should consider its appropriateness to your own financial situation, objectives and needs. The author and publisher are not liable for any loss caused, whether due to negligence or otherwise arising from the use of, or reliance on, the information provided, directly or indirectly, by use of this book.

The tools described in this book are provided for your information and to illustrate scenarios only. All reasonable care has been taken to prepare and design the tools.

A note on products

In order to provide objective general advice only, I have refrained from naming or recommending specific products or providers.

A note about figures

All figures in this book were correct at the time of writing, but things often change in the world of money, including the thresholds that apply to being able to receive, or having to make, various government payments. For the most up-to-date figures, check www.moneysmart.gov.au

FOR HOLLY AND DAISY,
AND FOR TEENAGE
GIRLS, EVERYWHERE.

YOU AND YOUR MONEY

Money. Like it or not, it's a big part of life, Queens. You'll need it to do many of the things you're dreaming about, whether that's to own the latest smartphone, wear the coolest clothing brands, buy a car or travel.

Chances are that you've received money from somebody at some point, and you might even have some savings from birthday money or other occasions. And one day all of you will earn some money of your own! The age you can start working varies around Australia, but when you hit 15 or so, you can get an after-school job. Or, you might start earning money doing things like babysitting, dog-walking, umpiring junior sport or selling things you make. All of a sudden, you'll go from having limited access to money to earning more than $50 a week (and, in some cases, quite a bit more). Sounds great, right?

It is! And having a job as a teenager gives you a whole lot more than money: through working, you'll learn life lessons and new skills, make new friends and gain experience to put on applications for other jobs. The hard part is knowing what to do with your extra cash.

You might be thinking, '*That's no problem: I'll spend it. There are so many things I want to buy!*' But when it comes to money, it's easy to make a lot of mistakes when you suddenly go from having none to having some.

However, knowledge is power, and that's where this book comes in. I'm here to walk you through some of the basics of money management, such as budgeting, tracking your spending and how to save.

It doesn't take long to get the hang of these things, and they are tools you can use for the rest of your life, no matter how much money you earn or how much your expenses grow. Because it doesn't matter how much money you have, it's what you do with it that counts.

I'll also explain some of the choices you'll be faced with on your money journey, such as how credit cards and buy now pay later services work; what you need to know now about education costs if you study beyond high school; where to start if you're thinking of investing; and how to use superannuation to save for your future.

If you think this sounds a bit boring, stop and read the sentence below. Then say it out loud. This is your new mantra, and it's the reason why this book is important:

MONEY MANTRA

Money is the key that will unlock my dreams. Learning how to look after my money is an important step in learning how to look after myself.

Queens, I've packed as much info as possible into this book so that you'll be armed with the knowledge you need to manage your money well and set yourself up to live your dreams, whatever they may be!

YOU'VE GOT THIS!

MEET YOUR GUIDES

I'm here to guide you on this journey, but I've also got a few friends along for the ride to help me. Meet Amina, Cam, Mai and Bella. They all identify as girls, they all live in Australia, and they all have questions about money. But that's where their similarities end. Each has her own goals, dreams and attitudes to money. They'll be popping up to ask questions and share their stories to help you rule your money like a Queen.

Amina's 15 years old and is in Year 9 at school. She's just landed her first job working at a supermarket. She's smart with spending and always shops the sales, but she's trying to get better at saving money as she wants to buy a car as soon as she's 18. She's loud, funny and always the life of the party. Amina loves dreaming up new ideas that could change the world and she wants to create her own start-up one day – she loves taking risks!

Cam's 14 and in Year 9 with Amina. She doesn't have a job yet, but she can't wait to get one! Cam loves having money and has saved up almost every dollar of pocket money or birthday money she's ever received. She's already saving to buy her first home! When it comes to taking risks, she's the opposite of Amina and prefers the safety of the sidelines over putting herself out there.

Mai's 18, works part-time at a juice bar and is in the first year of a Bachelor of Engineering at uni. She still lives at home. Mai likes spending money and now that she's old enough, she's started experimenting with using debt – such as buy now pay later services and credit cards – to pay for things. She's quite influenced by what her friends do, although she also knows how to think for herself.

Bella's also 18. She took a gap year after high school and she's about to start studying a Diploma of Beauty Therapy. She's a great saver and has spent the past year working full-time so that she could save up to buy a car and put a bit of money aside. She's also just moved out of home and in with her boyfriend. Bella hopes to own her own beauty salon one day, and she's focused on using her money to make her dreams come true.

CONTENTS

WHY IS THIS BOOK FOR GIRLS ONLY?

So far everything in this book is just as relevant to boys as it is to girls. So, you might be wondering why this book is only for people who identify as girls. The simple reason is that while gender equality has made great leaps forward since the days when women couldn't vote or get a job, men and women are still not equal when it comes to money.

Queens, it's crazy but true that being female can have an impact on how much money you could earn in your lifetime and the kind of retirement you'll be able to enjoy when your working life is over.

Closing these gaps and levelling the playing field when it comes to women and money is something that I'm passionate about – it's the very thing that inspired me to write this book in the first place.

YOUR MONEY INFLUENCES

I've found that there are four key influences that have an impact on how people feel about money.

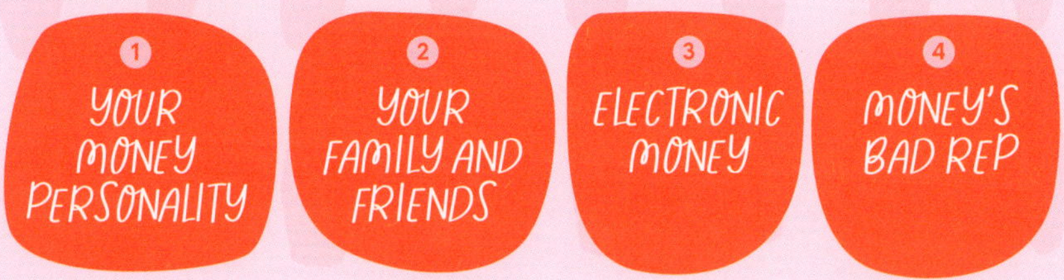

Your money personality

Your money personality, sometimes called your 'money mindset', is the idea that your personality affects your attitude towards money.

Take my family, for example: I have three kids and you might assume they're all good with their money given that they have a direct line to my advice on a daily basis. Not so. Two of my kids are impulsive and their money seems to flow out faster than it flows in. My other child is more considered in her approach to life and, as it turns out, to money.

In my experience, there are four main money personality types:

Quiz:

To work out which one you are, take the money personality quiz!

Q.1 You and a friend are throwing a surprise party for your bestie. You:

- **A** Spend all the money you have and splash out on a cake, chips, balloons, hats, party poppers – the works. She's your bestie, after all.
- **B** Make a list of what you need to buy and investigate how much each item costs. Cut the list so it fits what you've got to spend and split the costs 50/50 with your mate.
- **C** Get everyone who's coming to chip in $5: that way you can throw an awesome party without having to pay for it all yourself and dip into your savings.
- **D** Tell your friend you only have $5 to spend (even though you have $30) and let her pay for the rest.

Q.2 Your Grandma gives you $50. You:

- **A** Hit the shops the same day. After buying lunch, lollies to share with your friends, a face cleanser and a cheap T-shirt, it's all gone.
- **B** Jump online to compare prices for that cute $40 top you've been eyeing off. When you find it for $35 you buy it, happy that you've saved $5.
- **C** Add it to the money you've already got saved up towards a ticket to see your favourite band when they next tour.
- **D** Take it straight to the bank to deposit into your account. The buzz you get when you see your bank balance grow beats buying something from the shops every time.

Q.3 A movie you've been dying to see is released at the cinema. You:

- **A** Book tickets for you and your bestie (your shout) and treat yourselves to a large popcorn and drink combo at the cinema.
- **B** Invite your bestie, but you each pay for your own ticket and take snacks from home.
- **C** Check the cinema website, along with the internet, for any deals or discounts, and only go to see it if you find an offer or discount code.
- **D** Skip the cinema and wait until it comes out on Netflix (which your folks pay for) instead.

Q.4 Your favourite celebrity, who normally only wears designer brands, is photographed wearing a $20 shirt. You:

- **A** Buy it in all five colours available.
- **B** Buy one in your favourite colour.
- **C** Think about buying it but decide to save the $20 for your future car instead.
- **D** Encourage your bestie to buy it (in your favourite colour) so you can borrow it.

Your money personality type

MOSTLY A'S

SPLASHY SPLURGER

You spend money quickly and impulsively: considered spending or patient saving is not for you. You often regret your purchases and most of the time you're broke.

MOSTLY B'S

SAVVY SPENDER

You don't mind spending money, but you'll consider your purchases carefully. You'll shop around for the best deal or wait for the sale to make your money go a little further.

MOSTLY C'S

SUPER SAVER

You're focused on your own money goals. Instead of spending on cheap purchases, you'd rather set your sights on an expensive item and save up for it, or buy second-hand.

MOSTLY D'S

STINGY SQUIRREL

Although it sometimes means missing out, you'll say no to activities if they involve spending money. You're happiest when the money in your bank account is growing.

There are upsides and downsides to each money personality type. While Splashy Splurgers might find saving hard, they're often very generous with their money and are happy to spend it on friends or donate to charity. And Stingy Squirrels may have lots of money, but this often comes at the expense of missing out on some of the fun. The aim with managing money is to find the balance between spending and saving, splurging and squirrelling.

Your family and friends

After your personality, the second biggest thing to affect your attitude to money is the influence of your family and friends. You've been learning about money for years without even realising it!

As a kid, I didn't know much about money, but I knew that managing it and making the most of what you had was important.

We weren't rich – in fact, we were far from it – but when I was 12, my parents built a new house in the suburbs. For the first two years, we had concrete floors. This wasn't because they were trendy like they are today, but because we couldn't afford to install carpet. This taught me that if you can't afford something, you save up and wait until you can afford it, rather than buy it using something like a credit card.

The influence of your family and friends will be different from mine, but it'll definitely affect your attitude to money. For example, if you live with two parents or guardians who are always worried about money and even argue about it, you might think of money as something stressful. Or, if you have a friend who always has lots of money and splashes cash around, it can be easy to want to do the same, even if you don't have as much.

There might not be anything you can do about these influences, but it's worth having a think about who or what they are and acknowledging that they will have an impact on your attitude to money.

ACTIVITY **What do your money influences think about money?**

- Make a list of the people you spend most of your time with, such as your parent or guardian, siblings and friends.
- Thinking back to the quiz, try to guess their money personality based on how you see them spend and hear them talk about money.
- Get them to take the quiz for themselves.
- How close were you?

Electronic money

I know this'll make me sound really old, but when I was at school, money was physical. People carried coins and notes around with them, and most things – especially small purchases – were always paid for in cash. (But in those days, you could actually buy something with a 5 cent piece, like a chocolate button from the corner shop.)

Handling money definitely made it easier to understand and care about. One day your wallet was full, the next day it could be, quite literally, empty. Handing over a significant amount of money for something special you'd saved up for felt like a big deal, especially as you could see the cash you were parting with *and* what you got in return (your purchase). This also made it easier to understand the value of money and what things actually cost.

These days, tap and go is common, even for small items, which means you have to imagine the money being transferred from your bank account to the shop's bank account. Electronic money, or e-money, has made money harder to understand because we no longer handle it every day. In fact, you can complete the whole cycle of earning money and spending it without ever actually seeing or touching that money.

YOUR BOSS TRANSFERS YOUR PAY FROM THE COMPANY BANK ACCOUNT INTO YOUR BANK ACCOUNT.

YOU CHECK YOUR BANK BALANCE USING ONLINE BANKING.

YOU GO TO THE SHOPS, BUY AN OUTFIT AND PAY USING TAP AND GO.

In this example, it can be easy to feel like you got something for nothing, because you never physically handled the money. While e-money is definitely more convenient, it's also made the value of money harder to understand.

ACTIVITY **How well do you understand the value of money?**

- Take a look around your bedroom and make a list of all the major items, like your bed, desk, lamp and whatever else you might have.
- Have a guess at what you think they cost to buy.
- Check how you went by asking your parent or guardian what those items actually cost or by looking their prices up online.
- How close were you?

Money's bad rep

Money has a really bad reputation. Sure, people like earning it and spending it, but beyond that, many people think anything to do with money is boring and complicated. If I had a dollar for the number of times that I've heard women – young and old – say that money is too complicated to understand or that they can't be bothered thinking about it, I'd have a lot more money to be managing today!

Before I started writing about money, I also thought of it as complicated. But now I know better. Money itself isn't complicated – in fact, it couldn't be simpler. First, you earn it. Then, you use it to buy things you need or want. It's the financial system that exists around money that makes it complicated, mainly because there are lots of rules and technical terms involved.

However, once you understand a few basics and get beyond the technical terms, which I'll translate into plain English for you as we go along, it's pretty straightforward. It's worth investing just a little bit of time to understand money, because managing your finances is one of the most important life skills you can have.

You might be thinking you don't have to worry about money until you're earning more of it, like when you get your first full-time job. But when it comes to money, time matters. The habits you form when you're young will affect the relationship you have with money as you get older, so let's get started!

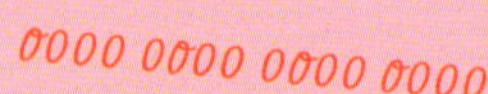

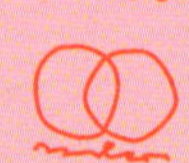

KNOWLEDGE IS POWER

Queens, it's time to get mad. It frustrates me to have to tell you this – and it may shock you to hear it – but while lots of progress has been made in the past 50 years when it comes to gender equality, this progress does not apply to women and money.

As outrageous as they sound, these are, unfortunately, the facts:

- Men earn more money than women at work.
  This is known as the gender pay gap.
- Men retire with more money than women.
  This is known as the gender retirement gap.
- In relationships, some men use money to exert control over women.
  This is known as financial abuse.

ARE YOU SERIOUSLY SAYING THAT MEN EARN MORE MONEY THAN WOMEN?

It isn't true in every single case, but when we look at the averages across Australia, that's exactly what I'm saying. It might be hard to read, and it might make you really angry, like it makes Amina angry, but it's important to understand why this happens, and how you can help bring about change for yourselves, your sisters, your friends, and even your future daughters and granddaughters. Because when it comes to money, knowledge really is power.

What is the gender pay gap?

You might be just starting to think about what you'd like to do for a career one day, like Amina and Cam, or imagining the fabulous life you'll be able to live when you have your first full-time job, like Mai and Bella. But before you start, here's something you need to know: on average, Australian women working full-time earn 13.8% less than Australian men.[1]

'But that's not fair!' I can hear you shouting. And you're right: it's not! And the truth is, we're just not making any progress. The gender pay gap is a problem all around the world and it hasn't changed much for the past 20 years.

The gender pay gap unpacked[2]

We'll get to *how* you can tackle the gender pay gap soon, but for now let's have a look at *why* the gender pay gap still exists.

Reason 1:
Women do different types of jobs than men, and the jobs we do pay less

As you know, there are no such things as 'women's jobs' and 'men's jobs'. But in some types of work there are more women than men, and vice versa, and these types of jobs are sometimes referred to as 'pink jobs' and 'blue jobs'. If you look at the table below, you'll notice that many of the jobs listed in the pink column involve caregiving or work based on helping others. Now compare this to 'blue jobs', which are typically done by men.

'Pink jobs'	'Blue jobs'
Nursing	Construction
Teaching	Mining
Social work	Trades
Child care	Manufacturing
Customer service	Transport
Administration work	Agriculture

So, now that we know the idea of 'pink jobs' and 'blue jobs' still exists, and that these jobs are linked to stereotypes about men's and women's roles in society, the next thing to understand is why 'pink jobs' typically pay less than 'blue jobs'. And the answer is: it all boils down to history – and sexism!

Women have been viewed as homemakers throughout history, which meant that when they first began leaving the house to do paid work (which was as recently as the 1940s), they were viewed as less capable than men. They were paid less money than men (even when they were doing the same job!), there were some jobs they weren't allowed to do, and they often had to stop working once they got married!

Queens, we know that we can do anything and are just as capable as men, but work-based gender discrimination is still widespread, and 'pink jobs' are still undervalued and tend to be lower paid than 'blue jobs'.

Mind the gap!

Reject gendered job stereotypes! If you hear someone labelling jobs as either 'pink' or 'blue', let them know that they are only reinforcing outdated gender stereotypes. And when you're considering your future career options, don't limit yourself based on ideas about jobs for men or women. Want to become a farmer? Great! An engineer, like Mai? Super! A tradie? Why not? The Prime Minister? Absolutely! And it's totally fine if you're like Bella and you want a job that has always been viewed as 'pink'. Just make sure you're aware of the impact it could have on how much you earn and, if you can, push for change by challenging how much these jobs pay.

ACTIVITY **Is there a gender pay gap in your family?**

- Ask your parent or guardian how much they each get paid.
- If you have two and one earns more than the other, ask them why.

Reason 2:
There are fewer women at the top

It probably won't surprise you to learn that men dominate the most senior positions in 'blue' industries, where the workers are mostly men. But what's shocking is that they also dominate the most senior jobs in 'mixed' industries, where the workforce is evenly split between men and women. And what's downright outrageous is that they dominate the top jobs in 'pink' industries, where the workers are mostly women, too!

Businesses with women in charge[3]

Having fewer women in top jobs not only means there are fewer women earning the same higher salaries as men but it also lowers the average amount of money women earn compared to men overall. And it means there are fewer women who have the power to promote other women to the top.

All of this is important because it can change how society values the jobs women do.

The barrier that stops women from rising to the top jobs is referred to as the 'glass ceiling'. Why do you think it might exist?

I'll give you a few main reasons.

- **Hiring bias:** this is when someone (e.g. a male executive) hires a person that reminds them of themselves (e.g. another man). Whether they're aware of it or not, they have a hiring bias.
- **A lack of flexibility:** leadership jobs are less likely to allow for flexible working or family-friendly hours, which many women need (or want) to balance work and family commitments. As Bella will be her own boss after she opens her beauty salon this is less likely to be a problem for her and she can help others by offering her staff flexible working hours.
- **Self-belief:** women can be pretty bad at valuing and recognising their skills. This makes us less likely to put ourselves forward for leadership jobs, thinking (wrongly) that we're not qualified enough. Even though she's still at high school, Cam is a little bit like this. She's really smart and all of her friends tell her she should run for the Student Representative Council, but she lacks self-confidence and doesn't think she would do a good job.

Mind the gap!

Queens, always have confidence in your ability! If a great work opportunity comes up, believe in yourself and go for it! If you aspire to have a senior role, aim for it. Once you make it, don't change to fit into the system – change the system to make it better for you, the women you work with and those who will come after you. Remember, it's the leader who makes the rules! And if you end up having a family and you're worried about how you'll combine more responsibility at work with family commitments, or if you're met with opposition from those in charge, challenge your bosses to make your situation work for you (and other women)!

Reason 3:
More women take time away from work or work part-time to care for others

Amina says she doesn't want to have kids, Cam and Bella aren't sure and although Mai is quite keen on having some, she's never thought about who will look after them and the impact that might have on how much she earns over her lifetime.

Do you think you'd like to have kids one day? If so, do you think that you and your future partner (if you have one, that is) should share the load when it comes to looking after them? Or do you think you'll want to take time out from work or work less to look after them? There's no right answer here – life should be all about choice! But this is another situation where knowledge is power.

Remember when I mentioned that women have always been viewed as caregivers? The reality is that the burden of caregiving still falls mainly on women. That's right – even today! What does that look like? More women than men: take parental leave (both paid and unpaid) after having a baby; work part-time to care for kids or other family members; or work fewer hours because the responsibility of doing household chores like washing, shopping, cooking and cleaning lies with them.

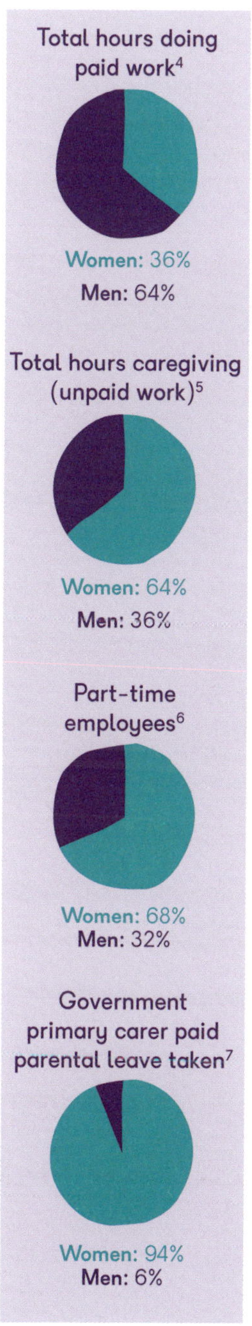

This is sometimes by choice, but it's often about the expectations of society, or families, or financial realities. If your partner is male and earns more than you, it's less likely he'll be the one to step back from the workforce and look after the kids. But when women do less paid work and more caregiving, we're less likely to advance in our careers as fast as men, or to rise to become the leaders in our industries (and enjoy the higher pay that comes with the top jobs!).

Mind the gap!

After seeing these stats, Amina is even more set than ever on never having kids. But if you're like Mai and you're certain you want to have them, keep in mind how you'd like to balance caregiving and working in your life and be aware that your decisions may impact your earnings. Why don't you ask your mum, aunt, grandmother, sister or female family friends if they have any advice for you?

I know decisions about looking after kids might feel like a problem for the future, but there are things you can do right now that will affect your life, and the lives of other women, later on. Firstly, if you notice that the boys and men in your life leave housework and caregiving to the women, challenge them to step up! Questioning whether your dad, brothers or other male relatives do their fair share of cooking and housework is a great start! Demanding fairness around housework and caregiving is something you can do later in life, too, whether it's ensuring male housemates take equal responsibility in a share house, a male partner does his fair share of the childcare or your brothers help care for your parents as they age. And if one day you have sons, teach them about gender equality from the day they're born!

ACTIVITY **Who does more caregiving in your family?**

- Ask your parent or guardian how they managed caring for you and working when you were little.
- If you have two parents or guardians, did one of them take parental leave or work part-time? If so, which one and for how long?
- And ask the women in your family how much unpaid care work they do compared to the men.

MONEY QUEENS TIP

EQUAL PAY IS DIFFERENT THAN THE GENDER PAY GAP

It's important to understand the difference between the gender pay gap and equal pay. The gender pay gap isn't the same as women and men with the same experience and qualifications being paid differently for doing the exact same job. That is illegal. If you ever find yourself in this situation, speak to your employer and, if necessary, you can take your complaint to the Fair Work Ombudsman.

What is the gender retirement gap?

Ok, Queens, stay with me here. I get that, for you, retirement probably seems about a zillion years away. In fact, it's so far in the future that it's probably never even crossed your minds – it's certainly something that Amina, Cam, Mai and Bella have barely thought about!

But one day, after a lifetime of work, you'll come to the point when you retire. Retirement sounds a bit like being a teenager but without having to go to school! You can spend all day, every day, doing anything you want – hanging out with friends, shopping, eating out, travelling ... but you know what else it sounds? Expensive. Why? Because you'll still have to keep paying for things even though you'll no longer be earning any money.

To help fund retirement, we save for it during our working lives. In Australia, this system is known as superannuation (or super, for short). You could begin earning super pretty much as soon as you finish high school (and possibly even earlier), so it's worth learning about it now.

Queens, unless you remember to rule your money, gender inequality is likely to follow you all the way into retirement. That's because men and women don't retire with the same amount of super. Instead, Australian women retire with 23.4% less money than Australian men, on average.[8] Welcome to the gender retirement gap.

The gender retirement gap in action[9]

There are a few factors that contribute to the gender retirement gap but, ultimately, the gender pay gap is responsible for most of them. We'll have a look at the main factors overleaf.

ACTIVITY **Is there a gender retirement gap in your family?**

- Ask your parent or guardian if they know how much money is in their super account. If they don't, maybe they could find out.
- If you have both a female and male parent or guardian, ask if they have a similar amount of money in their super accounts. What's the difference?

MONEY QUEENS TIP

SUPERANNUATION EXPLAINED

Super is a compulsory system of saving for retirement during our working years. It's one of the major sources of money for retirement in Australia. Having some super means that when we retire, we have some money to see us through the rest of our lives. Sounds pretty super, right?

Reason 1:
The way the amount of super you get is calculated

Every Australian worker aged over 18 has to have some money put into their super account by their employer. This money – known as the Super Guarantee – can't usually be accessed until they retire.

The minimum amount of money your employer must contribute to your super is calculated as a percentage of what you earn. The current amount is 10.5%, but in the coming years it will increase by 0.5% on 1 July each year until it reaches 12% in 2025.

How's the Super Guarantee calculated?

Annual earnings:
$50,000
a year

10.5% OF $50,000
= $5,250
in super from your employer each year

Because super is calculated as a percentage of what you earn, the more you earn, the more super you get and, as we know, women earn less money than men. In the past, not everyone received super. Previously, people who didn't earn more than $450 a month didn't qualify for the Super Guarantee at all – a policy that mainly affected women who worked part-time. Thankfully, this has now been changed, but it still has an impact on the amount of super today's women have access to. Super also isn't paid on government parental leave from work, which would mean that if Mai took this leave after having kids, she wouldn't get any super paid during this time.

These are yet more examples of the way the system is stacked against women. The result of these inequalities? Most women retire with less super than men.

Mind the gap!

Pay attention to your super and keep an eye on how much is in your account throughout your life. It also pays to look at more than just what you'll earn when you apply for a job. Some companies offer extra benefits beyond a high rate of pay, such as paying the Super Guarantee at a higher rate than the minimum required by the government or continuing to put money in your super when you're on parental leave. By considering all factors when you look for a job, you could give your retirement a substantial boost.

Reason 2:
Women put less of their own money into super than men

Under the rules of super, you can add to the payments made by your employer and put some of your own money into your super account in order to boost your retirement savings. (And if, in the future, you're self-employed or a contractor or freelancer, you can and should contribute to your super account, too!) But in order to put away extra money for your retirement, you need to have extra money in the first place. Knowing what we already do about the gender pay gap, it's little surprise that many women aren't able to find the extra money to do this. The result? By age 54, men have put an average of 37% more of their own money into their super than women.[10]

ACTIVITY **How does the gender pay gap impact the gender retirement gap in your family?**

- Ask your parent or guardian if they put extra money into their super.
- If they don't, ask them why not.

Mind the gap!

Try to put extra money into your super if you can. This might be especially worthwhile if you take parental leave or work part-time for a while, so that you don't fall behind. The rules of super also allow your partner (if you have one) to contribute to your super on your behalf, so this could be another option to help keep your super on track.

Reason 3: The way super investing works disadvantages women

The super that's put into your account doesn't just sit there until you retire. Instead, it's invested with the aim of making your money grow. Because you can't withdraw money from your super until you reach retirement, any profit on the money you have invested is reinvested, which helps your super to grow even faster. This is called compounding.

Compounding is most effective when your money is invested for a long period of time. What this means for your super is that you have the potential to make more money from the super that's invested early in your life. For example, the super invested in your 20s and 30s will likely grow into more money than the super that's put into your account and invested in your 40s and 50s.

The problem for women is that those younger years are exactly when some of us take time out of work or work part-time to have or care for kids. This limits the amount of super we accumulate during this time, which also limits its ability to grow – compared to a man's super – over the longer term.

Mind the gap!

Queens, knowledge is power and if you're aware of the astounding power of compounding, the time to focus on adding extra cash into your super is when you're younger. Luckily, this should also coincide with a time in your life when you have fewer financial responsibilities – you might even still be living at home with your parents. This is something Mai and Bella could start doing in a couple of years when they've finished studying. So, don't think of the gender retirement gap as a problem for future you – by taking ownership of your super from your 20s, you have the potential to set yourself up to retire in style.

Reason 4:
Men own more property than women do in Australia

Many Australians use property, such as owning a house or apartment, to help fund their retirement along with their super. For most property owners, it is the most valuable asset they have. When it comes time to retire, they can sell it and buy a smaller, cheaper property (known as downsizing) and use the extra money to help cover their expenses in retirement.

Fewer women than men own property in Australia, which is also a factor that contributes to women having less money to live off – and less secure housing – than men in retirement. It's a shocking fact and, quite frankly, a national shame that homelessness among women aged 55 and over is growing faster than in any other group in Australia.

Property ownership in Australia[11]

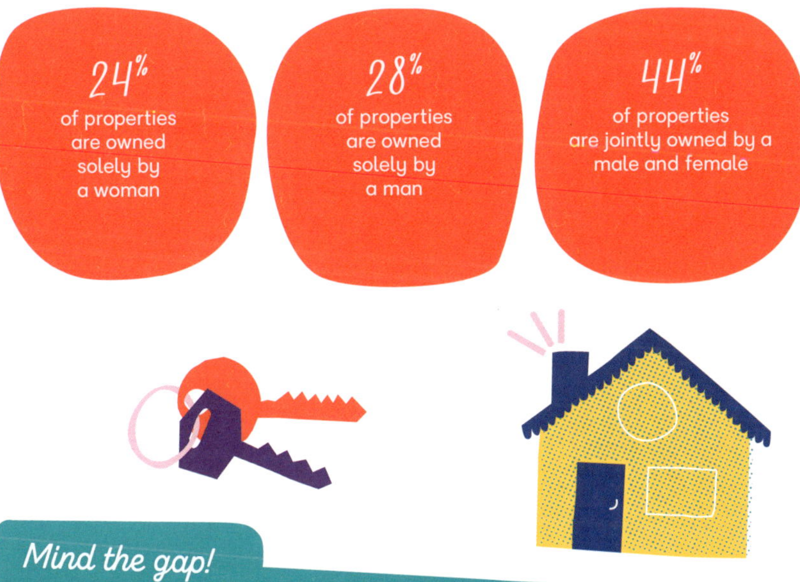

Mind the gap!

Property in Australia is among the most expensive in the world, and you'll probably have to save up really hard to be able to afford a deposit. We know that Cam is already saving to buy her first home! While 15 years old might feel too early to think about saving for a deposit, you could start thinking about whether you could save up to buy a property when you get your first full-time job. To make it more achievable, you could consider buying a property with a friend or relative. History tells us that property is also a fairly solid investment and a good way to grow your wealth. And, at the very least, it will mean you have somewhere to live and may not have to face homelessness in retirement.

'THE REALITY IS THAT IF WE DO NOTHING, IT WILL TAKE 75 YEARS, OR FOR ME TO BE NEARLY 100, BEFORE WOMEN CAN EXPECT TO BE PAID THE SAME AS MEN FOR THE SAME WORK.'

– EMMA WATSON

'I TRULY BELIEVE THAT WOMEN SHOULD BE FINANCIALLY INDEPENDENT FROM THEIR MEN.

AND LET'S FACE IT, MONEY GIVES MEN THE POWER TO RUN THE SHOW. IT GIVES MEN THE POWER TO DEFINE VALUE.'

– BEYONCÉ

QUEEN B IN CONCERT

FINANCIAL ABUSE AND HOW TO SPOT IT

Ruling your money is so important, Queens, and not just because it gives you the best chance of fulfilling your dreams. It could also save you from becoming a victim of financial abuse.

Amina's not alone here – plenty of people have never heard of financial abuse. Do you know what it is? Let's have a guess! Do you think it's:

- When someone stops you from accessing your money?
- When someone negatively influences your decisions about money?
- When someone uses your money without your consent?

If you thought it was any of these – or all three – then bingo, you're correct! Financial abuse includes all of the above and it's recognised as a type of domestic abuse. Financial abuse can happen to anyone, in any sort of relationship. But as a woman, you're twice as likely as a man to be financially abused.

How common is financial abuse in Australia?[12]

15.7% of women have experienced financial abuse

7.1% of men have experienced financial abuse

Financial abuse isn't well understood or taken very seriously. Considering nearly 20% of Australians don't think it's a serious problem, it's likely that it's much more common than the statistics show.[13]

Like all types of abuse, financial abuse usually starts small and can be hard to recognise at first. By the time many women realise it's happening, it can be difficult to escape from. So, the best safeguard is to always be cautious, and even a bit suspicious, when it comes to giving your financial power to others.

The red flags of financial abuse

Financial abuse is when someone ...

- Stops you from working and earning your own money.
- Controls your bank accounts, credit cards and cash, and doesn't give you access to these.
- Insists that you're paid into a bank account that only they have access to.
- Makes you ask permission to spend your own money.
- Checks or monitors what you're spending and punishes you for spending money.
- Refuses to contribute to shared costs, such as bills and household expenses.
- Forges your signature on financial documents.
- Forces you to sign financial documents you don't understand.
- Withdraws or transfers large amounts of money from your bank account.
- Uses your credit card without your permission.
- Takes out loans or credit cards or accumulates debts in your name without your permission.
- Pressures you to take out a loan or take on a debt on their behalf.
- Makes you feel guilty or threatens, hurts or punishes you if you don't give them money.
- Makes you feel stupid about money or that you can't be trusted with it.

MONEY QUEENS TIP

FINANCIAL ABUSE ISN'T ALWAYS ABOUT MONEY

It might sound confusing, but financial abuse isn't always about money – it's often about power and control. Some people like the idea of controlling someone else or making their victim dependent on them, because it makes them feel more important. This is vital to understand as financial abuse is sometimes used by perpetrators as a stepping stone to other types of domestic abuse.

I JUST MOVED IN WITH MY BOYFRIEND! WE SPLIT THE COSTS OF ALL OUR BILLS BUT HE TAKES CARE OF PAYING THE PROVIDERS. HE ALSO SUGGESTED WE GET A JOINT BANK ACCOUNT FOR HOUSEHOLD EXPENSES. IS THIS FINANCIAL ABUSE?

It's fantastic that Bella and her boyfriend have agreed to split the costs of their bills. And if she would prefer not to deal with paying the providers, it's great that her partner is happy to take on this responsibility. Go team! But if she's uncomfortable with this arrangement, and would like to be more involved, she must make sure she tells her boyfriend.

A joint bank account is a big step and something to carefully consider. Bella and her boyfriend should discuss some ground rules, like how much money they'll each put into it, and exactly what it can be used for, before they decide whether or not to open a joint account. Bella might also like to ask her family and friends for some advice about this.

Ultimately, none of the above information suggests financial abuse is present in Bella's relationship, but by giving control of some of her money to another person, Bella is opening herself up to some risk. She should always ask questions so that she knows how her money is being used, speak up if she's unhappy about it, and listen to her instincts if the situation doesn't seem quite right.

Queens, I know this is heavy, but there's really no way to sugarcoat it. The truth is that, as young women, you are at an even higher risk of financial abuse, especially if you:

- Don't understand money.
- Don't understand what financial abuse is.
- Don't recognise financial abuse as a type of abuse.
- Believe that men are in charge in relationships.
- Believe that a partner making financial demands on you is the price of love.

The good news is that just by reading this book, the chances of you being a victim of financial abuse should significantly decrease, because – remember – knowledge is power! When it comes to avoiding financial abuse, keep the following mantra in mind:

MONEY MANTRA

I will not give my financial power to someone else.

ACTIVITY **Who has the financial power in your household?**

- If you live with two parents or guardians, ask them who manages the money in your household.
- If they share the responsibility, how do they split it up?
- How did they decide who would do what?
- Ask them if there has ever been a time when they had to reclaim control of their finances from someone else. How did they manage it?

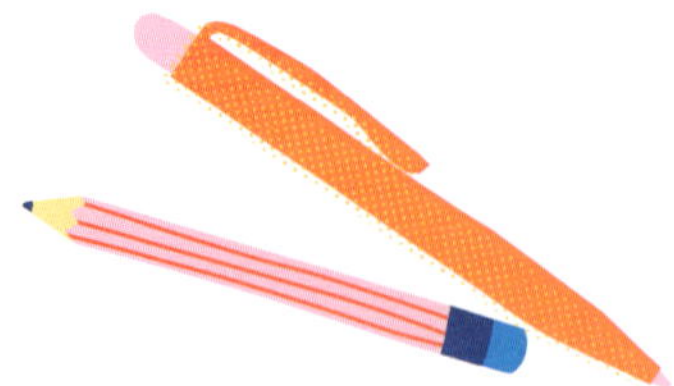

Five more ways to avoid financial abuse

1. Check your bank and credit card transactions regularly. If something seems out of place, start asking questions!
2. If you lend someone money, write down how much and when they'll pay it back before you give the loan (even if it's a family member!).
3. Don't give anyone access to your bank account details or debit or credit cards, and store financial and personal documents, logins and passwords in a safe place.
4. Always read and make sure you understand any financial documents you're asked to sign. If you don't understand, ask a friend or family member for help.
5. If you decide to combine your money with someone in the future, keep a separate bank account of 'dash cash', with enough money to get you out of a sticky situation.

GETTING YOUR FIRST JOB

If all this talk about ruling your money has got you motivated to go out and start earning some of your own, that's great! But if you don't have a job yet, you might be wondering how to go about getting one ...

Where to begin

Start by asking family and friends if they know of anyone hiring teenagers in your local area, or visit local businesses and ask if they're currently hiring. If you're going to do this, it'll help to be polite and look presentable. You could also follow companies you're interested in working for on social media, as many businesses post about job vacancies on their socials. Many companies will also post job openings on the 'Careers' section of their websites, so keep a lookout on these and on job search websites too.

You don't need to have already had a job to get another one (although it can really help). After all, everyone – even the most successful CEOs – once had a first job and started out somewhere!

Writing a CV

To apply for most jobs, you'll need to have a document called a 'résumé' or 'CV' (short for curriculum vitae), which lists your contact details and any skills or experience you might have that are relevant to the workforce.

If you want to know what a CV looks like, have a look at Amina's on the next pages. To get started on your own, download a free template from www.moneyqueens.com.au, or use a template in Microsoft Word or Google Docs. Most employers require your CV to be emailed to them or uploaded to their websites, but it doesn't hurt to print a few copies to hand out to businesses nearby, too.

CASE STUDY

Amina's CV

As you know, Amina recently landed a job at a supermarket chain. Check out her CV, with some explanations I've added about how each section helped her get the job.

Amina Agrawal
16 Smith Lane
Smithville
Phone: 3408 888 888
Date of birth: 01.01.2007

This info shows that Amina lives locally, is old enough to apply for a job, and lets prospective employers know how they can contact her.

About me:

I'm currently in Year 9 at Smithville High School. I'm a very enthusiastic learner and my biggest strength is my willingness to keep trying until I understand a concept or achieve a goal.

This section tells prospective employers a little bit about Amina and outlines some of the strengths that she might bring to the job, such as enthusiasm and a willingness to work hard and learn.

Availability:

I'm available to work Wednesday afternoons from 4pm-9pm and Sundays from 9am-9pm.

This lets prospective employers know when Amina is available to work, so they can easily see if her availability matches their needs.

Work experience:
Babysitting (since 2020)

I have done lots of babysitting for my parents, looking after my younger brother and sister, and I also babysit for other families in the local area. My responsibilities include: arriving on time, keeping the kids safe, giving them meals, putting them to bed on time and ensuring their parents return to a tidy home.

Here, Amina is letting prospective employers know she has some previous work experience, and that she understands the responsibilities that come with having a job.

Extracurricular activities:

- Netball – this has taught me the importance of working together as a team.
- Debating – this has taught me about time management and teamwork.
- Dance – this has taught me about how hard work can lead to improvement.

This part shows prospective employers that Amina has a range of skills that have been put to use in different situations, and that she's aware of how the skills she's learned through these activities, like teamwork and time management, could help in the workplace.

Awards/achievements:

Smithville High School – Commitment to Learning Award (Year 8)
Smithville Netball Club – Best Teammate Award (2020 and 2021)

This provides evidence that some of the things Amina has written previously, like being willing to learn and being a good team player, are true.

References:

Ms Sarah Villadella
Netball Coach
Smithville Netball Club
Ph: 3461 111 111

Mr Arjun Singh
Family friend and babysitting client
Ph: 3403 333 333

Prospective employers can call these people who know Amina well to check that the information she's provided is true. How these references describe her will help employers decide if Amina has the skills needed for the job, so be sure to give the names of people who will say good things about you – and ask them if it's ok first!

What's good about this CV is that Amina has demonstrated that she has the key skills that employers are looking for in teenage workers, such as:

- Reliability
- Punctuality
- Responsibility
- Willingness to learn
- Ability to work as part of a team
- Enthusiasm
- A good attitude.

Once Amina submitted her CV to the supermarket, she was contacted about coming in for an interview with the store manager. Amina turned up on time (in fact, getting there a few minutes early never hurts) and looked clean, neat and well presented (because first impressions really do count). The interview went well. Amina answered the manager's questions with her trademark confidence, repeating the points she'd made in her CV. And – obviously – she landed the job!

The top five things to do when you land a job

Once you land your first job, five things should be on your to-do list.

1. **Open a bank account**

   Your employer will ask for your bank account details so that they can pay you (yay!). You might already have a bank account, but if you don't, there are lots of things to consider when opening one. Check out pages 78 to 83 for more information about what these are and how to open one.

2. **Apply for a tax file number**

   Every worker in Australia has a personal tax file number. You probably won't be paying tax just yet – if you earn less than $18,200 a year (which works out to $350 a week), then you're not required to pay it. But you'll still need to give your employer your tax file number so they don't have to take tax out of your pay. Even if you don't find a job just yet, you'll need a tax file number to pay for study beyond high school, so it's worth getting one now anyway. Applying for a tax file number is free and pretty easy. You can find out how to do it on the Australian Taxation Office website. Read on for more info about what tax is and how it works.

3. **Talk to your parent or guardian**

   Now that you're earning some money it's possible your parents' or guardians' expectations might have changed around what they'll pay for and what you'll need to pay for yourself. There could be things they expect you to pay for now, such as your own phone bill or public transport costs, or you might be expected to contribute some of your pay to help out with household expenses. And if they previously paid you pocket money, find out if they'll still be paying it.

4 Set up a budget

Now that you've got some money coming in (and, depending on the talk with your folks, possibly some expenses, too) you'll need to set up a budget so that you can start to rule your money. I explain how to do this, and why it's really important, on pages 54 to 57.

5 Pay attention to your pay

If you want to make sure you're being paid fairly and correctly, you can check online at the government's Fair Work website. And it's always a good idea to check that the right amount of pay is being deposited into your bank account, rather than relying on your employer to get it right. To do this, keep a record of the hours you work, whether in a diary or an app, especially if your shifts change from week to week. Then check your payslip or bank statement against the hours you worked to make sure you've received the right amount of money.

Becoming a taxpayer

You've probably heard the word 'tax' but you may not know exactly what it is. Tax is money that workers pay to the government, which the government then uses to pay for many important things we share as a community, such as hospitals, schools, public transport, roads, social welfare and defence.

How much tax each worker pays varies depending on how much money they earn. Once you earn enough money to start paying tax, your employer will calculate how much tax you have to pay and will deduct that money from your pay each week or fortnight, before your pay is deposited into your bank account.

WHAT'S A TAX RETURN?

At the end of every financial year (which starts on 1 July and ends the following year on 30 June) you'll need to submit something called a tax return to the government. This is a summary of:

- How much money you've earned
- How much tax you've paid
- Any tax deductions you might be claiming, which help to reduce the amount of tax you have to pay.

In some cases, your tax return may show that you've not paid enough tax, which means you'll have to pay some extra, but in other cases your tax return might show that you've paid too much tax and some of that money will be refunded to you. If you want to find out more about tax and tax returns, head to the Australian Taxation Office website.

YOU'VE GOT THIS!

GIVE YOUR MONEY A GLOW UP

You might not have a lot of money right now, but you're still in control of what you do with the money you have. So, what do you want to do with it? You can spend it, obviously, but you can also save it, especially if your dreams for the future are big ... and expensive! Knowing how much to save and what you can afford to spend can be tricky, but it's worth learning because, Queens, knowledge is power. The best way to see what you can afford to save and spend is with a budget.

MONEY QUEENS TIP

UNDERSTANDING NEEDS VERSUS WANTS

There's a big difference between things you *need* to spend your money on, and things you *want* to spend your money on. 'Needs' are things that are actually required for your survival, like food, water and housing. 'Wants' are things that are nice to have, like the latest sneakers *everyone* is wearing. They might be cool but they're not actually essential to your survival!

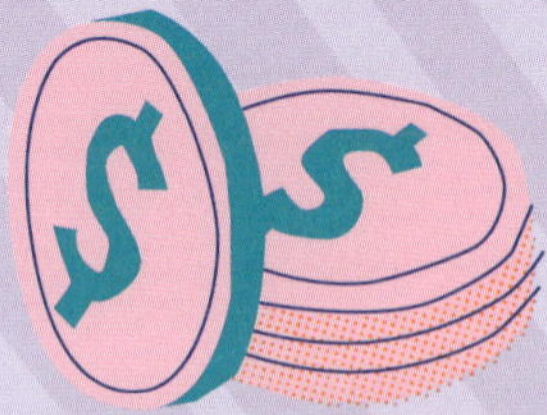

HOW TO BUDGET

Setting up a budget might sound a bit complicated or boring, but it's really just about having a plan for your money. It puts you in charge of your money, instead of your money being in charge of you.

Most budgets are monthly, but yours can be weekly or fortnightly if that suits you better. To set one up, you'll need to know the money you get on a regular basis (your income) and what you need to spend it on (your expenses). It doesn't take long to do, and once you've done it it's easy to update, which you should do whenever your income or expenses change.

CASE STUDY

Amina's monthly budget

Amina just got her first job, so this is the perfect time for her to set up a budget to track her income, her expenses and what she has left over to save up or to spend on things she wants.

Amina's income includes the money she is getting paid by the supermarket and the pocket money she gets from her parents for chores she does around the house. But now that she's working, Amina has to pay for her own mobile phone data as well as a weekly lunch from the school canteen. By adding in her income and her expenses, Amina's monthly budget looks like this:

Source of income	Amount	Type of expense	Amount
Earnings from work	$140.00	Mobile phone data	$20.00
Pocket money	$60.00	School lunches	$40.00
Total income	**$200.00**	**Total expenses**	**$60.00**

TOTAL INCOME − TOTAL EXPENSES = SPARE MONEY

Thanks to her budget, Amina can easily see how much money she has coming in and going out in needs spending. And by subtracting her expenses from her income ($200 – $60 = $140), she knows she has $140 of spare money each month, which she can save or spend on things she wants.

The expenses in Amina's budgets may be relatively small today, but as she gets older they'll grow to include things like groceries, bills, rent and maybe streaming services and a gym membership. By starting to budget now, Amina is putting good money habits in place that she'll be able to use as her income and expenses grow.

ACTIVITY **Create your own budget**

- To create your own budget, use the free download from www.moneyqueens.com.au or a free spreadsheet computer program like Google Sheets.

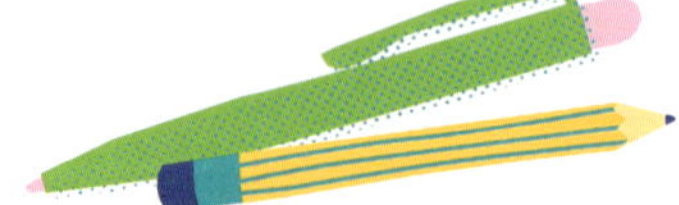

MONEY MYTH

YOU HAVE TO BE GOOD AT MATHS TO MANAGE MONEY

You don't have to be good at maths to manage your money. Sure, you'll need to use some maths, but this is one of those times when using a calculator is absolutely fine!

HOW TO TRACK YOUR SPENDING

I'VE GOT A JOB, SO WHY DO I FEEL LIKE I HAVE NO MONEY?

If you have a job, get pocket money, or even get birthday money, then you do have some money. People who say they have no money usually just don't know what they spend it on! Once you set up a budget and start tracking your spending, you'll figure out where it goes, and then you'll likely have more money than you realised.

The next step in Amina's money glow up is to figure out what she spends her spare money on after she's paid for her needs each month. Having so much money has been a novelty, and Amina knows she's been a bit spendy, but she wants to be smarter about how she spends her money in the future.

Tap and go payments have made money feel invisible, which can mean it's harder to monitor how much you're spending, but one easy way you can track your spending is to keep a money diary.

CASE STUDY

Amina's money diary

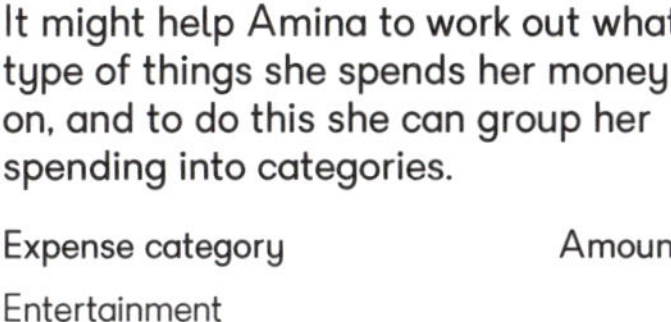

If Amina kept a money diary for a month, it might look something like this:

Expense	Amount
Saw a movie	$17.00
Large popcorn and drink combo	$15.00
New T-shirt	$19.95
New jumper	$45.50
Block of chocolate	$4.60
Açaí bowl	$13.00
New sunglasses	$24.95
Total spent	**$140.00**

If you remember from Amina's budget, she had $140 in 'spare' money each month after her regular expenses had been subtracted from her income. Her money diary shows that she spent all of her spare money, and what she spent it on. For Amina, spending all her money is a problem because she won't be able to buy a car when she turns 18 if she isn't saving any money at all.

It might help Amina to work out what type of things she spends her money on, and to do this she can group her spending into categories.

Expense category	Amount
Entertainment	
Saw a movie	$17.00
Entertainment total	**$17.00**
Food/drink	
Large popcorn and drink combo	$15.00
Block of chocolate	$4.60
Açaí bowl	$13.00
Food/drink total	**$32.60**
Clothes	
New jumper	$45.50
New T-shirt	$19.95
New sunglasses	$24.95
Clothes total	**$90.40**
Total wants spending ($17.00 + $32.60 + $90.40)	**$140.00**

Amina can now see that she has a bit of a problem with new clothes. As a Savvy Spender, she always shops the sales or looks for a discount, so she's a little surprised to see just how much she spends on them.

And ... repeat.

For Amina to get a really good understanding of her spending habits, she keeps a money diary to categorise her spending for a few months in a row so she can see if there are any patterns. After doing this, she realises it's definitely new clothes that are her weakness. And when she looks back at what she's bought over the last few months, she also realises she doesn't like – or wear – most of the things she bought just a few months ago. It dawns on her that if she wants to be able to buy a car, she might need to reassess the way she buys clothes and how much she spends on them.

ACTIVITY **Track your spending**

- Track your own spending for a month or more by using the free download from www.moneyqueens.com.au or a free spreadsheet computer program like Google Sheets.

How to spend like a Super Saver!

Super Savers, like Bella, still spend their money on things they want – they're just a little bit more considered in how they do it. So, Amina asks Bella for some advice. Bella says that instead of buying something on the spot, she waits 24 hours and if she still wants it, only then does she think seriously about buying it. But first, she checks the internet for discount codes or sales coming up. And she checks out second-hand marketplaces online to see if she can find the same item for less.

Thrift shopping is on the rise in Australia and it's a great way to buy unique, one-of-a-kind pieces that no one else will have, or snag an absolute bargain. You can also sell good quality or expensive items second-hand too, if you've outgrown them physically or emotionally, and make a little money back to save or spend on something else. Not only that, but it's much better for the environment to recycle and reuse, rather than spending money on fast fashion. And it's also better for your conscience. Because those cheap clothes are often made by girls and women working in unsafe conditions for incredibly low pay in developing countries.

Another Super Saver tip is to look for a job working for a company whose products you really like. Not only will it make going to work more enjoyable, but most companies also offer their employees a staff discount on their products. And when it comes to less fun spending, like public transport or mobile phone plans, check for student discounts or concession cards you might be eligible for.

So, Queens, the next time you're considering a purchase, ask yourself: 'What would a Super Saver like Bella do?'

MONEY QUEENS TIP

BUT EVERYONE ELSE HAS ONE!

It's normal to want to do the same things as your friends, whether that's listening to the same music or spending your money the same way. But everyone's money situation is different. Some friends have jobs while others don't; some may have to contribute money to household expenses while others might not have to pay for anything; and some may get lots of pocket money while others get none. When you're making plans, ensure no one feels left out simply because of money. Picnics, catching up for walks or just hanging at each other's houses are all cheap ways to spend time with your crew. And when it comes to what you do with your money, remember that the choice is yours alone. Learning to resist peer pressure is a big part of growing up and money gives you a great opportunity to practise this life skill!

HOW TO SAVE MONEY

Now Amina's got a budget in place and a clear picture of the money she has coming in and what she spends it on (both her needs and wants), she can begin to think about saving. And so can you! Start by making a list of the things you'd like to be saving for.

Maybe you want to save up for one big thing, like Amina and her car, or you might want to save up for several things such as:

- Schoolies or gap year travel after year 12
- A new phone
- A concert ticket to see your favourite band play live.

Look online to research what those items cost and think about whether there's a deadline for your savings. For example, it's no good saving enough to see your favourite band play in two years' time if their concert is next year!

If you have a savings goal in mind, the next step is to see whether your goal is realistic. For example, if you're saving up for your first property and you'd like to buy it when you're 20, the reality is you're probably not going to earn enough to achieve that goal by that deadline. So, what you can afford to save will really depend on your income and expenses.

If there's nothing you want to save up for right now, Queens, that's ok, but saving is a good habit to put in place and starting now will give you a head start when there's something big you want or need in the future.

ACTIVITY **What are your savings goals?**

- Make a list of your own savings goals, the amount you'll need and your deadline by using the free download from www.moneyqueens.com.au or a free spreadsheet computer program like Google Sheets.

CASE STUDY

Amina's savings goals

After researching the price of used cars and speaking to her family about the type of car that might suit her best, Amina decides she'll need to save $4,500 for it. And given she's just turned 15, she's got three years to get the money together!

Item	Cost	Deadline
Car	$4,500	Three years (Amina's 18th birthday)

For Amina to reach her goal of saving $4,500 in three years (or 36 months), she needs to be saving $125 a month ($4,500 ÷ 36 = $125). It's possible that she could do this – if you look back at her budget you'll see that after she'd paid for her needs she had $140 spare. But, as we saw from her money diary, Amina also likes spending money on things she wants as well. If she saves $125 a month for the next three years, she'll get her car, but she'll have to be a total Stingy Squirrel in the meantime. She'll only have $15 a month to spend however she wants, which is likely to be hard for someone with her personality, and might see her fail to achieve her savings goal.

As I mentioned earlier, the trick with managing money is to find a balance between spending and saving. It's important to be realistic about your savings goals – when people set themselves unrealistic goals, they're more likely to abandon them than reach them.

MONEY MYTH

I DON'T NEED TO SAVE – I DON'T CARE ABOUT BEING RICH!

Saving, or managing your money at all for that matter, is not about getting rich. But it could well be about not being poor. Not everyone is going to do the kind of job that earns them a lot of money, but if you're careful with the money you do have, you can make the most of what you've got.

Finding the balance

As you will have learned by now, the secret to any successful budget lies in finding a balance between saving and spending. To help find that balance, some people use a 'savings rule' to help them work out how much of their money they should be spending versus saving. There are a few different savings rules, but if you're still living at home, the one that might suit you best is the 30/30/40 rule.

The 30/30/40 rule

30% of your income should be spent on NEEDS

30% of your income should be spent on WANTS

40% of your income should be SAVED

CASE STUDY

Amina tries the 30/30/40 rule

If Amina split her income using the 30/30/40 rule, it would look like this:

Amina's total monthly income: $200.00

Needs	30%	$60.00
Wants	30%	$60.00
Savings	40%	$80.00

Now she compares this to how she's actually spending her money based on her budget and money diary:

Amina's total monthly income: $200.00

Needs	30%	$60.00
Wants	70%	$140.00
Savings	0%	$0.00

Amina is spending 70% of her income on wants, which is well above the desirable 30%. So, just as she had thought, if she wants to save enough for a car she'll need to cut back here, from $140 to $60 a month.

Amina decides she can live with this. She'll need to cut back a bit on the entertainment and treats and turn into a bit more of a Super Saver when it comes to shopping for clothes, but she'll still have some money for fun. And she calculates that if she saves $80 each month towards her car, she'll have saved $2,880 after three years ($80 x 36 months = $2,880). She won't have saved the full amount of $4,500, but if she adds any birthday or Christmas money she might get in the next three years, plus pay rises at work or extra shifts in the school holidays, plus any interest she might be able to earn on her savings (more on that soon), Amina's goal of buying herself a car for her 18th birthday seems like it could be within reach.

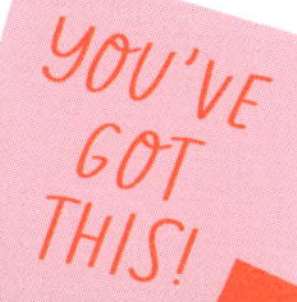

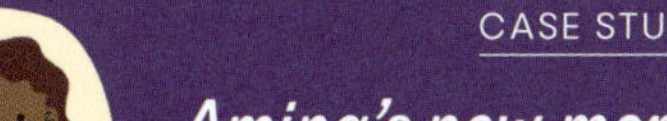

CASE STUDY

Amina's new monthly budget

Now that she's got her spending and saving sorted, Amina updates her monthly budget.

Source of income	Amount	Type of expense	Amount
Supermarket job	$140.00	*Needs spending*	
Pocket money	$60.00	Mobile phone data	$20.00
		School lunches	$40.00
		Needs total	**$60.00**
		Wants spending	
		Entertainment	$20.00
		Food/drinks	$10.00
		Clothes	$30.00
		Wants total	**$60.00**
		Savings	
		Car	$80.00
		Savings total	**$80.00**
Total income	**$200.00**	**Total expenses**	**$200.00**

Whenever things change for Amina – such as if she picks up another weekly shift at work, gets a new job or has to pay for new expenses – she should adjust her budget to make sure she's still on track.

ACTIVITY **Add your savings to your budget**

- Using your budget, money diary and the free download from www.moneyqueens.com.au or a free spreadsheet computer program like Google Sheets, calculate your needs, wants and saving percentages. How close are you to matching the 30/30/40 rule? What would your money split look like if you wanted to stick to the rule?
- Next, decide what spending/saving balance would work best for you and create your new monthly budget.

Different types of saving

Saving up to buy something you want is really just delayed spending – it isn't the kind of saving that will increase the amount of money you have. To do that, you'll need to save with the aim of increasing your bank balance.

Another kind of saving is 'saving for a rainy day' – something you might have heard adults say. Of course, they're not literally saving for a day when it rains! It's an expression that means they're putting some money aside for when things go wrong. In the future, such as when you move out of home, you'd be wise to do this too.

Bella has an 'emergency fund' with a few months of living expenses saved up from working during her gap year. This could really help if something unexpected (and expensive) happens, like she drops her mobile phone and it needs a new screen or if something bigger happens, like if her car needs an expensive repair or if she breaks up with her boyfriend and needs to find a new place to live. Whether it's 'dash cash' or a 'run fund' to help you escape an abusive relationship, or an emergency fund to protect you from unexpected expenses, having a safety net in the form of some savings behind you is really important as a woman.

MONEY QUEENS TIP

HOW TO STAY FOCUSED ON YOUR SAVINGS GOALS

If you're not very good at staying on track with goals, try writing them on sticky notes and placing them on your wardrobe door, or somewhere else in your room where you'll see them every day or create a mood board for your savings goals. There are other ways of staying motivated, too, like building in spending rewards as you hit financial targets along the way, or asking if your parent or guardian can match your savings or contribute some money when you hit milestones.

I RULE MY MONEY!

DREAM,
BELIEVE,
ACHIEVE.

RULING YOUR BUDGET

If you're like Amina, you've written your budget with your savings goals in mind and you have a good idea of how much money you have leftover for wants. But that's only half the fun! The rest comes down to tracking your spending against your budget. After all, it's no good having a budget if you're not going to follow it!

To see how you're tracking against your budget each month, you could add an extra column, called a 'spending tracker', where you can record your spending as the month progresses. You might like to update your spending tracker every time you spend some money or, at the very least, once a week. To get into the habit of doing this, it might help to do it at the same time each week, such as on a Sunday night.

CASE STUDY

Amina's new budget with a spending tracker

Amina has added a spending tracker column to her budget. This is how it looks halfway through the month.

Income		Expenses		Spending tracker
Supermarket job	$140.00	Mobile phone (need)	$20.00	$0 left (bill paid)
Pocket money	$60.00	School lunches (need)	$40.00	$20.00 left
		Entertainment (want)	$20.00	$13.00 left
		Food/drinks (want)	$10.00	$7.00 left
		Clothes (want)	$30.00	$10.00 left
		Car (save)	$80.00	$0 left (money saved)
Total income	**$200.00**	**Total expenses**	**$200.00**	**$50.00 left to spend**

By tracking her spending within her budget in this way, Amina always knows her financial position – how much she's spent and how much she has left to spend.

MONEY QUEENS TIP

SPLIT YOUR MONEY TO MAKE MANAGING IT EASIER

Each time you get some income in, the first thing you should do is separate your money, setting aside your savings, your needs spending and your wants spending. Having different bank accounts or bank accounts with sub-accounts can help with this, and I'll dive further into bank accounts in a minute. If you're dealing with cash, you can separate your money by putting it into different labelled envelopes or containers.

BANK ON IT

Bank accounts aren't just a place where you can store your money – they can be super useful when it comes to managing your money, too.

Opening a bank account

You might be able to open a bank account by yourself, depending on your age and the requirements of each individual bank, or you may need the help of a parent or guardian to open one for you. Either way, you'll need to provide the bank with various forms of ID like a birth certificate, passport, student ID or Medicare card to prove who you are.

You might already have a bank in mind because it's the one your parent or guardian uses, but it might be useful to ask them or another adult who's good at managing money to help you find out if their bank is going to be the best one for you.

If you can, try to do your own research, too! Many banks offer teen or youth accounts specifically for people between the ages of 13 and 18. Beyond the big banks, there are lots of smaller banks and credit unions, and sometimes these offer better deals.

A financial comparison website could help you compare the features of accounts from different banks side by side. But bear in mind that some companies pay to have their products promoted at the top of these websites, so look beyond the 'top picks' and 'sponsored links' to ensure you're comparing a wide range of products.

MONEY QUEENS TIP

LINK YOUR ACCOUNTS

As well as having a transaction account, which is what your employer deposits your pay into, you should consider opening a savings account. Make sure the two accounts can be linked so you can easily transfer your money between them!

Six things to keep in mind when you're choosing a bank account

1. **Fees:** Most banks charge fees in return for letting you have an account with them. These can include monthly account fees, withdrawal fees, ATM fees or internet banking fees. Whether it's a transaction account or a savings account, look for one with no fees if possible (or at least, very low fees).
2. **Cards:** To make tap and go purchases, and to get cash out at an ATM, you'll need an account with a debit card. If you want to be able to use your card for online shopping, you'll need a Visa or Mastercard debit card. This might sound like a credit card but it's not, as you can only spend money you have in your account. I talk about credit cards on pages 91 to 97.
3. **Apps:** Most banks provide their customers with access to a free banking app. The best apps allow you to do some of the things we've talked about already, such as tracking and categorising your spending, and setting up a budget and savings goals, which can make it easier to manage your money on a daily basis.
4. **Sub-accounts:** Some bank accounts allow you to open sub-accounts inside your main account. For example, you may have one savings account but open three sub-accounts that sit within it, one for each of your savings goals. This can be really useful to keep your savings for different items separate.
5. **Interest rate:** Any savings account will have an interest rate. This is what the bank pays you in return for you choosing to deposit your savings with it. (Check out page 82 for more info!) A higher interest rate will help your savings grow faster. But sometimes higher interest rates come with a catch, such as only applying for a short period of time, or requiring you to make a minimum monthly deposit or maintain a minimum or maximum balance. These days it's pretty hard to find an account that pays a high rate of interest, and if you do find one, make sure to check the details.

6. **Ethics:** You might also like to consider choosing an ethical bank that puts the planet and people ahead of profits. A quick online search will help you find banks that don't do business with companies that cause environmental or social harm, such as companies that produce firearms, tobacco or fossil fuels, or that make their money from gambling or live animal exports.

If you're not happy with the bank or bank accounts you've chosen, or you find a better deal, you can always change banks, which could save you money in the long run.

MONEY QUEENS TIP

YOU CAN SUPPORT OTHER WOMEN WITH YOUR FINANCIAL CHOICES

Did you know that you can support other women with your financial choices? When you're choosing your financial services providers, such as a bank or super fund, you could also look for those that support charities or social enterprises that are working to improve the lives of women. You could also do a little research into the support services that they offer women facing financial abuse or other domestic violence situations. After all, Queens, we're all in this together!

WHAT'S AN INTEREST RATE?

As Cam's such a great saver, she's really interested in finding the best savings account for her money. When you put your money into a bank account, you're effectively 'lending' your money to the bank. They pool all the money deposited with them to lend to other people or businesses, but your money is always available whenever you want to withdraw it.

In return for lending your money to the bank, the bank *pays you* interest on your money. The amount of interest you receive is calculated using an interest rate. As a simple example, if you deposit $100 into a savings account that pays 2% interest a year, the bank will pay you $2 each year ($2 is 2% of $100), bringing your account balance to $102 after one year.

Interest rates also apply when you borrow money from a bank, such as if you buy things using a credit card or take out a loan to buy a car or a house. In this case, the bank *charges you* interest in return for lending money to you. For example, if you borrow $10,000 from the bank, and they charge you 2% interest a year, you'd owe the bank $10,200 after one year ($200 is 2% of $10,000).

Money management apps

Beyond the app that comes with your bank account, there are also lots of apps that have been created by other developers to help you manage your money. These apps can do things like track and group your spending into categories, set spending limits for each category and send you a notification when you're approaching your limit. Like all apps, there are free and paid versions, but the free versions should do enough for you. If you decide to use one of these, make sure it can be linked to your bank accounts, so whenever you spend money the details transfer to the app automatically.

MONEY QUEENS TIP

THE SAFETY OF SAVINGS

One benefit of having your savings in the bank is that amounts up to $250,000 are 'guaranteed' by the government. This means that if the bank went broke, the government would make sure you got back all the money you had saved in there.

I WANT IT NOW: UNDERSTANDING CREDIT AND DEBT

Wanting to have something as soon as you see it and not being willing to wait has a name: instant gratification. It's the same thing Ariana Grande sings about in '7 Rings', but unless you've also had five platinum-selling albums, I'm guessing you probably can't afford to buy or do everything you want straight away. Or maybe you're more like Veruca Salt from *Charlie and the Chocolate Factory*, who didn't care how she got what she wanted, as long as she got it now! The problem is that the *how* part really does matter.

It's possible to have things we can't afford, and to get them as soon as we want them, thanks to credit cards and buy now pay later services. The result? People are no longer as willing to wait for things!

But, Queens, it wasn't always this way. When I was young, people saved up until they had the money to go to the store, buy the item and take it home. Or if they couldn't afford to buy something, they might have put it on lay-by, which is a system where you'd pay a deposit for an item and then pay off the remaining amount in regular instalments, interest-free. The item remained at the store until it had been paid for in full, and then – and only then – could you take it home. (Believe it or not, lay-by is still around today if you know where to look!)

The lowdown on buy now pay later

Buy now pay later services (also called BNPL) work the other way around from lay-by: you can buy what you want and take it home immediately, even if you don't have enough money to cover the cost of the purchase.

BNPL is particularly popular with people under 30. And, I get it, it's pretty attractive – why wait when you can just have what you want now? I'm guessing you've heard the saying, 'If something's too good to be true then it probably is'? Well, BNPL services can be exactly like that.

BNPL is a form of credit, and using it means you have a debt. In simple terms, this means that a BNPL company pays for a purchase on your behalf, and the cost of your purchase is then broken down into repayments that you make to the BNPL company. You usually have to pay the first of these at the time of checkout, with the other payments taken out of your bank account or deducted from your credit card at regular intervals until you've paid for the item in full.

BNPL fees explained

Instead of charging interest, most BNPL companies charge three types of fees:

1. **Late fees:** Customers who don't make their repayments on time are charged late fees. The amount varies among BNPL providers. Between 9% and 15% of BNPL transactions each month are hit with late fees.[14]
2. **Other customer fees:** Some BNPL providers also charge other fees, like account-keeping fees (typically around $6 per month); establishment fees when you open your account (which can be up to $90, depending on the cost of what you're buying); or transaction fees (typically around $3 per transaction).
3. **Retailer fees:** Retailers that offer BNPL are charged a fee of between 2% and 8% of the cost of each purchase. BNPL providers stop retailers from passing this fee onto the BNPL customer, so instead retailers spread these costs by increasing prices for all customers.

Getting a BNPL account

To use BNPL, you must be 18 years old. Most companies will ask for your email address, mobile phone number and debit or credit card details. Yes, that's all they ask for! It's fairly easy to get a BNPL account because providers don't check whether you'll be able to pay back the money you borrow, or if you've got BNPL debts with other companies. By comparison, banks are required by law to verify how much money you have, if you have a job and if you have any debts before they lend you money. This is to check that you'll be able to pay them back, and to decide whether to lend you the money based on your answers.

BNPL companies aren't legally required to ask these types of questions. And – to be honest – they don't *really* care about your financial situation. After all, if you have trouble paying them back, they can charge you late fees, which is one of the ways they make their money.

MONEY QUEENS TIP

THE POWER OF ADVERTISING

If you've seen BNPL ads, you might think it seems pretty great, and that everyone is using it, especially younger people. If you believe what you see, you might even think you'll be missing out or having less fun if you don't use it. But you're smarter than that, Queens. There's nothing fun about having stacks of debt – in fact, it's incredibly stressful and a sure-fire way to stop you from being able to live your dreams. So here's a new mantra for you ...

MONEY MANTRA

I rule my money, and I won't let marketing or advertising rule me.

CASE STUDY

Mai's first BNPL experience

Mai's 18 and is old enough to use BNPL. Mai works at the juice bar and earns $150 a fortnight. She is a Splashy Splurger and likes to buy things as soon as she sees them. When she finds an amazing dress online that costs $180, she wants it immediately – even though she only has $45 in the bank. So, Mai decides to try BNPL, which some of her friends use. The company takes the first payment of $45 out of Mai's bank account at checkout. Two days later, the dress arrives. But Mai still owes $135, or three more payments of $45.

Cost of dress: $180

1st repayment: $45
(due at time of purchase)

2nd repayment: $45
(due two weeks after purchase)

3rd repayment: $45
(due four weeks after purchase)

4th repayment: $45
(due six weeks after purchase)

Two weeks later

Mai's been sick and hasn't been able to work for the past two weeks, so her bank balance is still $0. The BNPL company tries to take the next instalment of $45 but it can't. Because Mai missed her repayment, she's charged a $10 late fee. The amount Mai owes for the dress has increased from $135 to $145.

Three weeks later

Mai still hasn't made the missed repayment a week later, so she's charged another late fee of $7, bringing the total amount she owes to $152.

Four weeks later

Mai's back at work and has been paid $150. A friend asks if she wants to go to the Ed Sheeran concert – the ticket price is $150. By this stage, Mai has worn the dress a couple of times and is a bit over it. She forgets she still owes money on it and pays her friend for the concert ticket. The next day she gets a reminder about her upcoming BNPL payment. Mai knows she doesn't have the money in her account but the late fees feel so small that she doesn't worry about it. When the BNPL company can't take the payment, she's hit with another $10 late fee, bringing the total she now owes to $162.

Five weeks later

There's still no money in Mai's bank account and, as she still hasn't made her second missed payment, she's charged another $7 late fee, bringing the total she owes to $169. She tries to buy some shoes using the same BNPL company, but because she's missed payments on the dress, they won't let her make another purchase. She considers using a different BNPL company to buy the shoes, but (thankfully) she decides not to.

Six weeks later

Mai picked up an extra shift at the juice bar this week, so instead of being paid $150, she's been paid $222. The next reminder pops up about her final BNPL repayment (which is now for the total amount of $169 as she's reached the end of the BNPL agreement). The company takes the full payment, leaving Mai with just $53 in her bank account.

Luckily, Mai had the money to make the final BNPL payment. If she hadn't been able to pay, the company would have closed her account and continued to contact her about making the payment. If she'd still not repaid them, they may eventually have passed her debt on to a debt collection company (a business that chases down overdue debts), which would have continued to pursue Mai for the payment. If you have bad debts, such as this one, the details are also sometimes passed onto a credit reporting company and they can have a negative effect on your credit rating (see page 90 for more on credit ratings).

In the end, the $180 dress – which Mai doesn't even like anymore and has given to her friend, Bella – cost her $214. Because she didn't read the BNPL agreement, she had no idea she would be charged late fees if she didn't make her repayments on time. Luckily, the BNPL company she used didn't charge account-keeping fees or transaction fees, otherwise the dress would have cost Mai even more.

Original cost of dress: $180

Amount Mai paid: $214

The result: Mai paid $34 (or 19%) more for the dress than she would have if she'd saved up and bought it with her own money.

Understanding credit ratings

A credit rating is a score based on your credit history. Once you're 18 or older, if you've ever had a credit card, entered into a contract like a mobile phone or gym contract, or, in some cases, used BNPL, you'll have a credit rating.

This credit rating, or score, is a measure of how likely you are to repay your debts in the future (known as your 'creditworthiness'). To calculate your credit rating, credit reporting companies monitor how often you've applied for credit, the amounts of money you've applied for and borrowed, and how good you are at paying regular bills or repaying your debts on time.

This score is used by banks when you want to borrow money for something really big – like a property. The higher your score, the better. The easiest way to make sure you have a high credit rating is to always make your payments and repayments on time. If you're ever wondering what your credit score is, credit reporting companies are required by law to give you access to your credit report and credit rating, if you request them.

MONEY QUEENS TIP

FROM LITTLE THINGS, BIG DEBTS (CAN) GROW

Small credit purchases can easily snowball into large debts if you're not careful. If you're thinking about signing up for a credit card or a BNPL service, always read the terms and conditions and work out in advance what fees you'll be paying on top of the cost of your purchases.

The lowdown on credit cards

Credit cards are another form of debt that lets you pay for things you don't have the money for. Like BNPL, you can use your credit card to make purchases and take them home or start using them straight away. The risks associated with credit cards are similar to BNPL, and in many ways they can be a lot worse as credit card debts can hang around for years and years!

Credit cards have been around for much longer than BNPL services and they work a bit differently. They're usually issued by banks and other lenders, such as credit unions. You might also see credit cards issued by airlines, supermarkets and other retailers, but in most cases they're working in partnership with a bank.

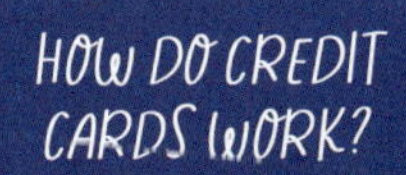

When you buy something and pay for it using a credit card, you borrow the money for your purchase from the credit card company, which pays the retailer on your behalf. The credit card company then charges you interest on your purchase. You have to make a minimum monthly repayment (which is usually around 2% of what you owe, or around $20 to $25, whichever is higher). There is no time limit on when you have to pay the credit card company the full amount back, but the longer it takes you, the more interest you'll pay.

Credit card fees explained

Credit card companies charge a combination of fees and interest.

1. **Interest:** Most credit cards come with an interest-free period (typically around 45 days). This period begins from the date of your monthly statement, which will tell you how much you owe, what the minimum monthly repayment is, and when that repayment is due. If you pay off the full amount within the interest-free period, you won't be charged any interest, but if you only pay the minimum monthly repayment, or pay more than the minimum but less than the total, then the remaining amount will have interest added to it. And – this is important – the interest rates that credit card companies charge are extremely high. For example, the average interest rate on a credit card is typically in the range of 13% to 22%.
2. **Customer fees:** These include annual fees and late fees if you don't make your repayments on time. It's also possible to use a credit card at an ATM to withdraw cash. But unlike the cash you withdraw using your debit card, which comes out of your bank account, cash you withdraw using a credit card is effectively a loan, and a cash advance fee, as well as interest, is charged on it.
3. **Credit card surcharges:** Credit card companies charge retailers who accept credit cards a fee of around 1% to 2% of the cost of each purchase. Retailers often pass this fee onto customers as a credit card surcharge.

Getting a credit card

Like BNPL, you can't get your own credit card until you turn 18. The process of applying and being approved for a credit card is a bit more involved than setting up a BNPL account. Generally, you'll need to provide information such as where you work, how much you earn, what credit limit you'd like, and any debts you have – which could include BNPL debts. The credit card company will also check your credit rating. Based on all this information, it will decide whether it wants to give you a credit card and, if it does, what your credit limit (the maximum amount you can spend using the card) will be.

Interest-free, flat-fee credit cards

One of the latest innovations in the world of credit cards is interest-free, flat-fee credit cards. These are aimed at younger customers who might instead opt for BNPL services. While there's no interest, which makes these credit cards sound appealing, they do still charge a fixed monthly fee. And just like with regular credit cards, you still have to make a minimum monthly repayment in addition to the monthly fee. The fee is calculated based on your credit limit but usually ranges from around $10 to $25 a month and is a fixed amount regardless of how much money you owe on the credit card. But if your balance is $0, and you make no purchases in a month, the monthly fee is refunded, making the card free to have for that month.

CASE STUDY

Mai's first credit card

Now let's imagine that instead of using BNPL, Mai decides to apply for a credit card. She is given one with the following features:

Credit limit:
$1,000

Annual fee:
$59

Interest rate:
14%

Minimum monthly repayment:
2% of her balance, or $20, whichever is higher.

We know Mai earns $300 a month at the juice shop. She'll be able to cover the minimum monthly repayment, which, at 2% of her total $1000 credit limit, would be $200 if she were to spend the full $1,000 credit, or less if she spends less. There's no way she'd be able to pay back her full credit limit of $1,000 in a month, but we know that's ok with the credit card company.

When Mai opens the account, the annual credit card fee of $59 is charged to the credit card. Then Mai sees the same amazing $180 dress and buys it with her credit card. She doesn't use the credit card again in the first month of having it.

One month after getting her credit card

When Mai gets her first statement at the end of the month, it shows she owes $239 ($59 + $180). She also has to make the minimum monthly repayment of $20. (You might be thinking that $20 is not 2% of $239. That's correct! 2% of $239 is $4.78, but this is less than the credit card company's minimum repayment amount of $20, so Mai is charged $20 instead.) Mai doesn't really understand how her credit card works and she didn't read the terms and conditions, so even though she earns enough to pay more, she assumes that all she has to repay is the minimum monthly repayment, and that's what she does. She now owes $219 ($239 - $20).

Two months after getting her credit card

Mai's been sick, so she hasn't been able to work and earn any money. She's now being charged interest on the money owing on her credit card. At the end of the month, her statement shows she's been charged interest of $2.35, so she now owes $221.35 ($219 + $2.35). Her minimum monthly repayment is $20, which Mai is unable to pay as she's not worked this month. But that doesn't stop her from paying for the $150 Ed Sheeran concert ticket on her credit card, increasing the amount she owes to $371.35! She's also charged a $20 late fee when she doesn't make a monthly repayment, so she now owes $391.35.

Three months after getting her credit card

When Mai's next monthly statement arrives, $4.65 more in interest has been added to what she owes, bringing the total to $396 ($391.35 + $4.65). Her minimum monthly repayment is still $20, which she pays, bringing the amount she still owes down to $376.

Four months after getting her credit card

This month, Mai's statement shows she owes $380.33 after being charged another $4.33 in interest ($376 + $4.33). Again, her minimum monthly repayment is $20, which, after she pays it, reduces what she owes to $360.33.

So far, Mai has paid $60 off her credit card, which has covered the annual fee, but she hasn't really even begun to repay the money she borrowed for the dress or concert ticket yet. On top of the cost of those two items, she's been charged $79 in fees ($59 annual fee + $20 late fee) and $11.33 in interest.

Let's skip forward ...

Two and a half years after getting her credit card, Mai hasn't made any more purchases on it. But she has continued to only ever make the minimum monthly repayment of $20, which, after that first late payment, she's always paid on time. It has taken her two and a half years to pay off her credit card in full, which has cost her $197 in fees (3 x $59 annual fees + $20 late fee) and $71.64 in interest.

Original cost of Mai's purchases: $330 ($180 dress, $150 concert ticket)

Fees charged: $197

Interest charged: $71.64

Total amount Mai paid: $598.64

Total time it took: 2.5 years

The result: Mai paid $268.64 (or 81%) more for her purchases than she would have paid if she'd saved up and bought the dress and concert ticket with her own money.

MY STORY:

THE TRUTH ABOUT HIGH CREDIT LIMITS

When I got my first credit card, my credit limit was $400. I wanted to have access to just enough money to get me out of trouble in case I couldn't pay the rent, or if my car broke down. (Queens, I should have had an emergency fund instead! But I haven't always been good with money ... at that stage I was spending all my money every week and not saving anything!)

I didn't put the credit card away for use in emergencies only – I started using it to buy things I wanted but didn't need and which I definitely couldn't afford.

I was an ideal customer for the credit card company: I always made the minimum monthly repayment, though I could never afford to pay any more, so the interest they were charging me kept growing, and so did the money they were making from me.

You might think that a bank would want to know if you'll be able to pay your card in full each month, but this is not what they're concerned with! The bank just wants to know whether you can afford the minimum monthly repayment on your credit limit. They're actually counting on you not being able to pay it off in full each month so you carry a balance forward, as that means they can charge you more interest and make more money. Because I was such an ideal customer, the credit card company offered to increase my credit limit to $1,000 (something they're not allowed to do anymore, thankfully!). I didn't even earn $1,000 a month at that time, and I had expenses like rent, food and petrol. There was no way I could afford to pay off $1,000 a month. Luckily for me, I sensed a higher credit limit could get me into real trouble, so I turned it down and stuck to my $400 limit. Even now, I have a pretty low credit limit compared to what I earn, but I also have an emergency fund and pay off my credit card in full every month.

So, Queens, if someone ever tells you they have a $20,000 credit limit, don't be impressed. That might mean they have $20,000 of debt, which is not something to brag about. The street cred, and your admiration, should actually go to the person who has a $0 credit card balance each and every month. Or, better yet, someone who doesn't have a credit card at all, because they're probably financially better off.

MONEY MYTH

YOU NEED A CREDIT CARD FOR ONLINE SHOPPING AND YOUR CREDIT RATING

It's not true that you need a credit card to shop online. A Visa or Mastercard debit card can also be used for online purchases. The difference is, these cards use the money from your own bank account to pay for your purchases instead of using the bank's money. It's also not true that you need a credit card to get a credit rating. As I explained, credit rating agencies monitor a whole lot of regular payments – not just a credit card. If you can't handle the responsibilities of a credit card, you'd be better not to have one than to have missed repayments affecting your credit score.

SALE

How to be smart with credit

I have a credit card and I've used BNPL (admittedly only for research purposes), so I'm not going to tell you that you should never use either (no, 'Do as I say, not as I do' here, Queens).

You'll sometimes see BNPL promoted as a budgeting solution and it's true that some people can use it, and credit cards, this way: they'll spread out repayments for an item over time without ever paying interest or late fees. But these people are the exception rather than the rule (and they're usually really, really good at managing their money and sticking to their budget!). The best budgeting solution is budgeting itself, and only spending what you can afford, when you can afford it.

If that doesn't sound like you, and you think you could be more like Mai, approach credit with caution! Remember, Queens, knowledge is power. Credit can be tricky and unless you know what you're doing, you can get into serious debt trouble using it.

The problem with credit

Top five risks of using credit

1. **It can create bad money habits**
   Using credit makes it easy to spend money you don't have, which can lead you to develop bad money habits, such as impulse buying, overspending or, in extreme cases, a spending addiction. These habits can be hard to break as you get older and can become more serious as the amounts of money you're able to borrow and spend increase.

2. **You'll be vulnerable if your circumstances change**
   Your debt will not go away, even if you cannot afford to pay it. Credit providers are required to offer hardship assistance if you're unable to pay back your debts due to a change in your life, like being unable to work due to illness or losing your job. But these are generally only temporary measures like pausing your repayments. When your situation improves, your debts will still be waiting for you.

3. **It can lead to a cycle of debt**
   People who get into trouble with debt often take on more debt to try to help them get out of it, such as taking out a credit card to cover BNPL payments and fees or taking out a loan to pay off credit cards. This rarely works and usually just makes the problem worse, and you'll end up owing more money.

4. **It can make it hard to borrow money in the future**
   This is a big one. When you want to borrow money to buy something substantial, such as a car or a property, one of the things lenders check is your outstanding debts and your credit rating. If your credit rating is low it indicates that you've previously misused credit by missing repayments, not paying on time or racking up late fees, which means there's a good chance they'll reject your application.

5. **It discourages mindful spending**
   Having to save up for something gives you time to stop and think about whether you really need or want it. If you're a bit of a Splashy Splurger, a good tip to stop impulse buying is to sleep on it. If you wake up the next day and still think you can't live without it, save up for it. The wait may make you appreciate it a little more. Buying things you've had to save up for encourages mindful spending and can give you a sense of satisfaction, reward and achievement, which can be good for your self-esteem.

Top five tips for using credit wisely

1 Understand what you're getting into

Be prepared to read a lot of fine print, Queens! BNPL and credit card companies all have different terms and conditions, some of which are only revealed in the fine print. To truly understand the way each service works, and the risks that come with using them, make sure you always read and understand each product's features and each individual company's terms and conditions before you use their money.

2 Start small

Rather than jumping in with a $500 BNPL purchase or a credit limit of $2,000, start small. That way, if you get into trouble with debt, it will only be a little bit of trouble, rather than a whole lotta trouble! If small debts can snowball into bigger ones, big debts can turn into an avalanche!

3 Always repay in full and on time

This is the golden rule of using credit. If you have BNPL or credit card debts, include them in your budget, make sure you know when your payments are due and prioritise them ahead of any wants spending. Some companies may send you reminders about your repayments, but plenty of them won't. Use an alarm or calendar app to schedule your own reminders about upcoming payments, and double-check that you have the money you need to cover them in your bank account to avoid late payment fees. And pay off your credit card balance in full by the due date each month to avoid interest charges. If you can't afford to do these things, you probably shouldn't be using credit in the first place.

4. **Have an emergency fund**

   Overspending on your credit card or BNPL might not be a true emergency, but it may be better to use your emergency fund to get you out of debt than to rack up interest and late fees. If you end up using your emergency fund to clear your debts, make sure you save hard to replace the money and treat this as a one-off event.

5. **Prioritise your debts and get help if you need it**

   If you get into trouble with debt, the first thing you should do (after you stop spending) is figure out which debts to pay first. These should be the debts with the highest interest rate, or the biggest financial penalties for missing repayments. To work this out, it can help to write all of your debts, payment amounts, due dates and penalties down. You should also contact the BNPL or credit card company to discuss the problem, as they might be able to change your repayment schedule, give you additional time to repay, or consolidate your debts into one payment to make them more manageable and save you money on fees and charges. Ignoring the problem will only make it worse, and certainly won't make it go away. If you feel the credit company isn't making a genuine effort to help you, you can make a complaint to the Australian Financial Complaints Authority, and if you need more help, you can contact the National Debt Helpline for free financial counselling.

MONEY QUEENS TIP

THERE'S NO SUCH THING AS FREE MONEY

Queens, remember that credit card companies and BNPL companies are businesses. They are not there to help you rule your money and fulfil your dreams. They operate to make a profit for their owners (their shareholders). Remember, *there's no such thing as free money.*

Social media influencers and credit

If you're anything like the teen girls I know, you follow some people on social media who look like they're living amazing lives. They're probably not much older than you, but their lives couldn't be more different. Have you ever stopped to wonder how they can afford to holiday at the nicest resorts, wear designer labels and have the latest ... everything? And if the answer is, 'Because they're a social media influencer!', do you know what that actually means?

You might already know that influencers are given free clothes, holidays or other products in return for promoting these things to their followers. Brands have them do this in the hope that you'll buy the products, which can also be a bonus for the influencer as they sometimes get a cut of the sales. It may seem that scrolling through their posts is pretty harmless. But, Queens, remember that they're benefiting from subtly convincing us that we need the things they're posting about. So, if you see that a social media post is 'promoted' or 'sponsored', remember that it's an ad trying to sell you something. And no matter how great these influencers make it seem, the chances are that what they're selling isn't going to make you more like the person promoting it. (And you probably don't need it!)

But what about people who don't seem like they're social media influencers? There are lots of young people flashing their fabulous lives on socials, and their posts aren't sponsored, so you might be wondering where their money comes from. In some cases, they might have wealthy parents who are funding their luxurious lifestyles. But in many cases, their bling is being funded by credit. In short, they're fake rich: they spend money they don't have to sell their followers the illusion of a dream life. In return, they attract more likes and a boost to their self-esteem. They might accumulate more followers, but do you know what they're also accumulating? A mountain of debt that will eventually come crashing down on them, leaving them broke.

Don't be fooled. It's not normal for a 20-year-old to be decked out head to toe in designer brands or holidaying at hotels that cost thousands of dollars a night. What's much more normal is for that same girl to still be living at home with her parents, working at a cafe, studying at uni and hitting up the sales at her local shopping centre. Or she might be renting an apartment with some friends while trying to establish herself in her first full-time job and saving up for a road trip down the coast.

So, Queens, just remember that in a lot of cases – and especially on social media – things are often not what they seem. Stay true to yourself and your dreams, and remember your mantra ...

MONEY MANTRA

Money is the key that will unlock my dreams. Learning how to look after my money is an important step in learning how to look after myself.

There is such a thing as good debt

After all the shade I've just thrown on credit, you might be surprised to hear that some types of debt are considered 'good debt'. Some examples are:

Borrowing money to **BUY A HOME,** which Cam is hoping to do once she's saved up for a deposit.

Borrowing money to **START A BUSINESS,** like Bella will need to do to open her own salon in a few years, or what Amina might need to do to get one of her business ideas off the ground.

Borrowing money to pay for **FURTHER EDUCATION** – Mai is already borrowing money from the government for her uni degree, and Bella will be doing the same for her diploma.

These debts are considered good debt because they have the potential to grow your wealth. For example, borrowing money to pay for your education (beyond high school) might feel expensive at the time, but it is an investment in yourself and in your future, and it might lead to different job opportunities and higher income later in life. Or, if you borrow money to buy a home and the property increases in value, you get to keep the extra money you make after you've paid the bank back. (And you also have somewhere secure to live in the meantime.)

This doesn't mean that good debt is risk-free. All debt comes with some risk; for example, the value of your property might not increase.

But by contrast, you're unlikely to make much money from clothes, make-up, sporting equipment, tech, entertainment, and other products or services you pay for using a credit card or BNPL. This is what's considered as bad debt. You could try to resell those things, but their value is unlikely to have increased in the time you've owned them.

Like the other examples of credit we've already learned about, the credit that funds good debt comes with terms and conditions of its own, which you need to be aware of before you commit to taking on this debt. And as with all credit, being on time with making the payments required will save you on extra fees and charges, and paying the debt off as fast as you can will save you from paying unnecessary interest.

'EVERY WOMAN'S SUCCESS SHOULD BE AN INSPIRATION TO ANOTHER. WE'RE STRONGEST WHEN WE CHEER EACH OTHER ON.'

– SERENA WILLIAMS

'MY HOPE FOR THE FUTURE ... IN EVERY YOUNG GIRL I MEET ... IS THAT THEY ALL REALISE THEIR WORTH. AND ASK FOR IT.'

– TAYLOR SWIFT

PAYING FOR LIFE BEYOND HIGH SCHOOL

No matter what school you go to, there's a good chance your parents or guardians have paid for your education so far, covering the cost of uniforms, books, fees and perhaps even the fun things like school camps and socials. But that's likely to change, Queens, once you finish high school. Whether you go to university, do vocational training, take a gap year or get a job, you're probably going to have to cover a lot more expenses yourself. So, let's take a look at some of these options and the costs that come with them.

Paying for uni

I am sure that some of you have your heart set on going to uni, whether it's to study a particular course or just for the experience. Many of you might have parents, guardians or other family members who are very eager for you to go, too. (And if they're anything like me, they've been telling you this for a while!) And there will also be some of you who are on the fence about going, or who feel that uni is not for you right now (or ever).

Regardless of whether you're going to uni now, planning for it in the near future or haven't decided yet, you need to know how much it could cost you, and how to factor this into your money plans.

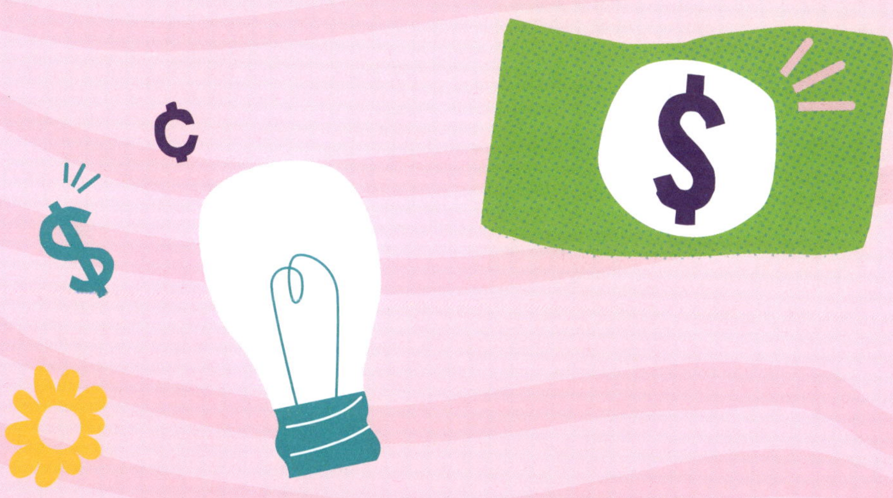

Attending uni isn't free, and different degrees cost different amounts. But if you're an Australian citizen or permanent resident, you will probably be able to get what's called a Commonwealth supported place (or CSP). This means the government will pay for some of the cost of your undergraduate degree and will lend you the money to cover the rest of the cost (which is known as the 'student contribution'). You'll never actually see the money you're lent in your bank account – instead the government pays it directly to the uni, and they'll expect you to begin paying it back through the tax system once you earn over a certain amount of money. (More on this on page 116).

Because you don't have to pay for your course upfront, it's easy to think of uni as free. (Although, you'll still have other costs like books and equipment to pay for.) You will graduate with a debt to the government, but as we discussed on page 104, it's a form of good debt because having a uni degree should enable you to earn more money and achieve some of your life goals and dreams.

Factors that'll affect how much uni costs

Exactly how much you'll pay for uni depends on what degree you study and whether you have a CSP.

Commonwealth supported places (CSPs)

CSPs are available to most Australians citizens and permanent visa holders studying an undergraduate degree at a public uni, as well as some of Australia's private universities and higher education providers. If you're studying at a private provider that doesn't offer CSPs, or if you're an international student, you can apply to attend uni as a full-fee paying student. Your acceptance letter will outline whether you've been offered a CSP.

If you're a full-fee paying student, you'll need to pay for the entire cost of your uni degree without the help of a government subsidy.

The degree that you choose

The exact amount uni will cost also depends on the degree you're studying and which subject units you choose within that degree.

To give you a rough guide, the table below shows the maximum cost of one year of full-time study for different degrees, for both CSP and full-fee paying students. To work out the approximate total cost of the degree you're interested in, you'll need to multiply this amount by the number of years it usually takes to complete the degree full-time.

The cost of different uni degrees per year[18]

UNDERGRADUATE DEGREE TYPE	Maximum cost for a CPS student per year	Maximum cost for a full-fee student per year
Education, English, Statistics, Mathematics or Clinical Psychology	$3,985	$17,354
Nursing, Indigenous Studies or Foreign Languages	$3,985	$20,381
Computing, Visual Arts, Performing Arts, Built Environment or Allied Health	$8,021	$21,390
Medicine, Dentistry or Veterinary Science	$11,401	$38,644
Commerce, Arts, Law, Accounting, Economics, Administration or Society and Culture	$14,630	$15,739

WHY DO DIFFERENT DEGREES COST DIFFERENT AMOUNTS?

In the past, the amount you had to pay for a degree was based on the lifetime earnings potential of graduates. For example, if you studied medicine or law, you paid more for your degree as people who become doctors and lawyers are among some of the highest paid in our society. But, Queens, the amount that a degree now costs is based on the skills the government thinks will be most in demand in the future workforce. For example, the government wants to encourage more students to study mathematics, science, nursing and teaching because they think there will be a future skills shortage in these areas. So, that's why these are among the cheapest uni degrees. But the costs that you see here could change in future if the government makes more changes to uni funding.

MONEY QUEENS TIP

UNI FRIENDS CAN BE FUTURE BUSINESS PARTNERS

Queens, uni isn't all about working hard so you can graduate and get a good job at the end ... socialising at uni can be very important, too, and not just because it's fun! In fact, some of the world's most successful young entrepreneurs met and formed the partnerships at uni that led to their financial success.

For example, Google co-founders Sergey Brin and Larry Page met at Stanford University in California, where they developed the online search engine; and later at the same uni, Snapchat was created as a class assignment by Evan Spiegel, Reggie Brown and Bobby Murphy. The co-founders of Canva, Melanie Perkins and Cliff Obrecht, met at the University of Western Australia, while TV and radio duo Hamish Blake and Andy Lee landed their first radio show after meeting at the University of Melbourne.

So, if you're a budding entrepreneur, keep an eye out for like-minded people at uni and dare to dream together.

Paying for vocational education and training

Not all workforce qualifications can be gained at uni – some qualifications are offered through vocational education and training (VET) providers instead. For example, you might need to do a VET course if you want to be a beauty therapist like Bella, or a fashion designer, electrician or chef, or if you want to work in child care, bookkeeping, fitness, construction, project management, real estate, interior design and many other areas.

These courses tend to offer more practical, hands-on training than uni degrees, and they are generally much shorter in length. Qualifications range from Certificate I to Certificate IV, all the way up to Diplomas, Advanced Diplomas, Graduate Diplomas and Graduate Certificates. You can study for a VET qualification through registered training organisations, such as Technical and Further Education (TAFE) institutes and private providers. The entry requirements for VET courses vary, but as a rule they're easier to get into than a uni degree.

MONEY QUEENS TIP

VET CAN PROVIDE ANOTHER PATHWAY TO UNI

A VET course might be just what you need to get your dream job. But some VET courses can also be used as a stepping stone into uni, too. Many universities around the country partner with VET providers to offer pathway courses, which will help you to get into a uni course later. So, Queens, if you don't get into the uni course you were aiming for straight out of high school, you might be able to get into uni later on via the VET system.

Factors that will affect how much VET costs

Exactly how much you'll pay for a VET course depends on what you study, where you study and whether you have a subsidised place.

Subsidised VET places

You can only get a subsidised place if the course you want to study is subsidised by the government. The government subsidises most courses offered by TAFEs, as well as many offered by private VET providers. Exact eligibility requirements differ across Australia but, generally speaking, to be eligible for a subsidised place you need to be an Australian citizen, permanent resident, humanitarian visa holder or New Zealand citizen and live in the state you want to study in. To find out if the course you're interested in is subsidised and if you'll qualify for a subsidised place, it's best to look online or contact the VET provider you'd like to study with directly.

If you don't qualify for a subsidised place or the provider you want to study with doesn't offer them, you can still complete a VET course as a full-fee paying student, which means you'll have to cover the entire cost of the course yourself.

The provider and the course that you choose

Fees for VET courses can vary quite a lot between different providers, even for the same qualification. This is because the fees are set by the individual providers and there are no regulated minimum or maximum costs. But shorter courses and lower-level qualifications usually cost less than those that run for longer or are more advanced.

If you have a subsidised place, the average amount the government will contribute is about 75% of the cost of the course, leaving you to pay the remaining 25%. On average, that's about $1,100, but there can be a lot of variation: fees for Certificate I qualifications are as low as $100 on average, while the average fee payable by the student for an Advanced Diploma is $3,400.[19]

It's best to look online or contact VET providers to find out the courses they offer, whether they are subsidised and what out-of-pocket costs you will have when you enrol. As with any purchase, shop around until you find an option that works for you.

Paying back your education loans

Queens, remember on page 110 when I said that the government can loan you the student contribution for your uni degree with the expectation that you'll pay it back through your tax? This is done through the Higher Education Contribution Scheme (HECS) Higher Education Loan Program (HELP), or HECS-HELP for short.

Similarly, if you have a subsidised place at a VET provider, and you're studying for a Diploma-level qualification or higher, you can access a government loan called a VET Student Loan (or VSL) to help you cover the additional fees.

When do I start paying back my education loans?

You'll start paying back your HECS-HELP or VSL debt once you're earning a certain amount of money. This is called the compulsory repayment threshold, and it varies slightly each year.

In the 2021–2022 financial year, you needed to have earned a minimum of $47,014 to start paying back your education loans. The more you earned, the more you paid back. For example:

- People earning between $47,014 and $54,282 paid back 1% of their income.
- People earning between $77,002 and $81,620 paid back 5% of their income.
- People earning over $137,898 paid back 10% of their income.

As these thresholds change each year, you should check the Australian Taxation Office website for the most up-to-date information.

How do I pay the government for my education loans?

Student loans are paid back through the tax system. The amount you have to repay is calculated by the Australian Taxation Office when you submit your tax return at the end of each financial year. Your employer may withhold money from your pay to count towards your HECS-HELP or VSL debt, essentially helping you to repay the debt a little at a time, so you don't end up having to find the money as a lump sum to make your repayment at the end of each financial year.

MONEY MYTH

I WON'T HAVE TO PAY BACK MY LOAN IF I DON'T GRADUATE

Queens, this isn't true. You will have to pay for any units of study you enrol in if you don't withdraw from them by a certain date (known as the census date). This applies even if you don't finish the units, don't pass the units or don't end up graduating with a qualification. You will begin to repay what you owe through the tax system once your income reaches the compulsory repayment threshold.

As Bella knows, if she was to borrow money from a bank or another credit provider, she'd usually have to pay interest on top of the amount she originally borrowed, which is the 'cost' of borrowing the money.

The good news is that the government doesn't charge interest on HECS-HELP or VSL debts. However, the amount you owe will increase over time to reflect increases in the cost of living in society. This is called inflation, and when it's added to your student debt (which happens on 1 June each year) it's called indexation. The amount of indexation applied each year will vary, depending on what's going on in the Australian economy. For the most up-to-date indexation rate, check the Australian Taxation Office website.

Getting an education loan

Providing you're eligible, getting a student loan is simply a matter of doing some paperwork. In fact, it's as easy as A-B-C!

B

GET A UNIQUE STUDENT IDENTIFIER (USI) NUMBER

(You can apply for one online!)

C

SUBMIT YOUR PAPERWORK BY THE CENSUS DATE

specified by the uni or VET provider

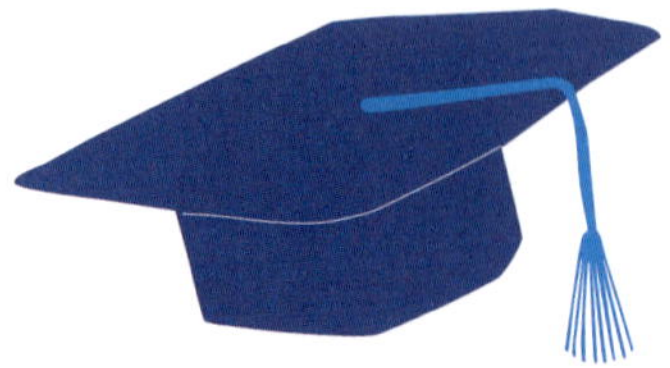

More handy tips about education loans

- **There's a minimum pass rate requirement for HECS-HELP**
  If you have a CSP for a full-time uni course and you fail more than 50% of your subject units in a year, you'll be at risk of losing your CSP and no longer qualifying for a HECS-HELP loan.
- **You can get a discount for paying for uni upfront**
  If you're able to pay your full student contribution amount for uni upfront each year (perhaps your parent, guardian or another relative is paying this for you!), you'll get a 10% discount on the cost of your uni degree. If you can't pay the full cost upfront, but you can pay at least $500 upfront each year, you'll get a small discount on the amount you borrow under HECS-HELP.
- **You need to prove you're still studying to remain eligible for a VSL**
  To remain eligible for a VSL, you'll need to complete something called a progression form twice a year.
- **Your student loan is repayable overseas**
  If you move overseas to live after completing uni or a VET course, you'll still need to make repayments on your student debt if you're earning above the compulsory repayment threshold, as you would if you were living in Australia.

CASE STUDY

*Mai's uni loan**

Let's fast forward three years – Mai recently graduated from uni after completing a Bachelor of Engineering degree and has landed her first full-time job as an engineer!

As Mai had a CSP at uni, she only had to pay for the part of the degree that the government didn't subsidise, which was $8,021 per year. Mai's degree involved four years of full-time study, so the amount she had to pay came to a total of $32,084 ($8,021 x 4). She used a HECS-HELP loan to pay this amount.

Straight out of uni, Mai got a job as a graduate engineer, earning $73,911 per year.[20] As she's earning more than the compulsory repayment threshold of $47,014, Mai needs to start paying back her HECS-HELP loan at the end of the next financial year.

The amount Mai needs to pay is 4.5% of her $73,911 income, which works out to be $3,326. Her employer has been withholding $63.96 to cover this HECS-HELP repayment from her pay each week during the year, so she's been able to make her repayments this way rather than having to find the full amount at tax time.

After the repayment has been made for the financial year, Mai checks her HECS-HELP balance and sees that she now owes $28,758 ($32,084 - $3,326).

On 1 June the following year, the government applies indexation of 1.8% to Mai's HECS-HELP debt. This increases the amount she owes to $29,276 (1.8% of $28,758 is $518, so $28,758 + $518 = $29,276).

At the end of that financial year on 30 June, Mai's HECS-HELP repayment is again calculated to be $3,326, as she still earns $73,911 and her repayment rate is still 4.5% of her income. Once deducted, this payment brings her HECS-HELP loan balance down to $25,950 ($29,276 - $3,326).

If nothing changes, and Mai continues paying the same amount off her HECS-HELP loan each year, it will take Mai another nine years to repay her loan, bringing her total repayment time to 11 years after finishing uni.

**Based on 2021–2022 repayment thresholds*

CASE STUDY:

*Bella's VET loan**

As we know, Bella took a gap year after finishing high school and then chose to study a beauty therapy qualification at TAFE. Let's fast forward a year to when Bella has graduated from her Diploma of Beauty Therapy and landed her dream job working as a beauty therapist full-time.

Bella chose a course and provider that offered a government subsidy. The full cost of her course was $15,500 but the government covered 75% of the cost (or $11,625), leaving Bella to pay the remaining $3,875. She was able to use a VSL to pay this amount.

Bella earns $53,664 in her first year of work,[21] and as she's earning more than the compulsory repayment threshold of $47,014, Bella needs to start paying back her VSL at the end of the next financial year.

Based on what she earns, Bella needs to pay the government back 1% of her $53,664 income – which works out to be $536.64. Her employer has been withholding $10.32 from her pay each week during the year to cover this repayment, so she's been able to make her repayments this way rather than having to find the full amount at tax time.

After the repayment has been made, she checks her VSL balance and sees that she now owes $3,338.36 ($3,875 - $536.64).

On 1 June the following year, the government applies indexation of 1.8% to Bella's VSL debt. This increases the amount she owes to $3,398.45 (1.8% of $3,338.36 is $60.09, so $3,338.36 + $60.09 = $3,398.45).

At the end of that financial year on 30 June, Bella's repayment is again calculated to be $536.64, as she still earns $53,664 and her repayment rate is still 1% of her income. Once deducted, this payment brings her VSL balance down to $2,861.81 ($3,398.45 - $536.64).

If nothing changes, and Bella continues paying the same amount off her VSL each year, it would take her another six years to repay her loan, bringing her total repayment time to eight years after graduating from her Diploma.

**Based on 2021–2022 repayment thresholds*

MONEY QUEENS TIP

YOUR CIRCUMSTANCES WILL CHANGE OVER TIME

Estimating how long it will take to pay off your student loans is tricky because a number of things are likely to change as time passes, including:

- The rate of indexation applied to your student loan each year.
- The repayment amounts required at different income levels.
- How much money you earn.

You might also choose to make additional repayments to pay off your student loan sooner. But, Queens, if you have the money to do this, you may want to consider paying off other debts that are costing you money in interest charges, rather than prioritising the repayment of your interest-free student loan.

MONEY MYTH

MY STUDENT LOAN LIMIT IS ENDLESS

Every person eligible for government education loans in Australia has a limit on how much they can borrow over their lifetime. This is known as the HELP loan limit and it's worth remembering if you switch courses a few times, or if you want to keep studying different courses from undergraduate to postgraduate levels. This limit changes slightly every year, but is currently just above $100,000 for most students, and a little higher for students in medicine, dentistry, veterinary science and some aviation courses. For the most up-to-date information on the HELP loan limit, visit the government's Study Assist website.

The HELP loan limit includes all VSL, HECS-HELP and FEE-HELP loans you take out (more about that last one in a minute!). When you repay the money you borrowed to study, these amounts are credited back to your lifetime limit – so if you want to do further study, and use the government loan system to pay for it, this could be another reason to pay back your student loans faster.

Paying for further education as a full-fee student

If you don't have a CSP at uni or a subsidised place with a VET provider and you're an Australian citizen (some New Zealand and humanitarian visa holders also qualify), there is another government loan scheme, FEE-HELP, to assist with paying for your qualification.

FEE-HELP works in a similar way to HECS-HELP and VSL, although in some cases there's an extra 20% fee added to the cost of each unit of study. Similar to HECS-HELP and VSL, FEE-HELP covers tuition fees only and does not cover other study-related costs, like books, equipment and accommodation. To continue to be eligible for FEE-HELP, you need to maintain a minimum 50% pass rate.

If you decide not to use FEE-HELP or don't qualify, some VET providers also offer the option to pay your fees on a weekly or monthly basis. Some offer private loans, but you'll need to read the terms and conditions carefully to see if there are any additional charges or if interest is involved.

MONEY QUEENS TIP

A SCHOLARSHIP CAN YOU HELP YOU PAY FOR YOUR EDUCATION

Scholarships are another option to keep in mind when you're applying for uni or VET. A scholarship can help you pay for your studies, in full or in part, and they're not just available to the smartest students. Most unis offer their own scholarships – you can find out more about who they're for, what expenses they cover and how to apply on their websites. Government and charitable scholarship programs are also available for both uni and VET studies. They are designed to level the playing field for students from all sorts of backgrounds, including Indigenous Australians, rural and regional students, minority students and those living with chronic illness, among many other groups.

HOW BIG A FACTOR SHOULD COST BE WHEN DECIDING WHAT TO STUDY?

Given the costs involved in further study, you might be like Amina and wonder how much you should consider those costs when you're deciding what to study and where.

Every person's situation is different, but it could help to think about education as an investment in you, and to weigh up the costs involved against how the course you want to study appeals to your interests, and how it will provide you with new skills and help you financially in the future.

To truly understand the value for money that different courses offer, and the impact they could have on your future earnings, you could research the average salaries for different jobs and also the job opportunities available.

It's also worth remembering that many people end up in careers that are completely different than what they studied. Some uni degrees are a pre-requisite for some careers, like studying medicine if you want to become a doctor, but other degrees are more general and could lead you to work in multiple industries.

Cost might be a factor to consider if you're trying to decide between two courses that could lead to the same career, but I suggest looking at all the other factors – like location, course duration and unit study plans – alongside cost to make your decision.

But, ultimately, if you study something that interests you, you're more likely to complete the course. And if you're going to spend the next 40 years working, I'm sure you'd rather be doing a job that you enjoy!

ACTIVITY **How did the members of your family decide what to study?**

- If your parent, guardian or older sibling did further study after high school, ask them if they considered the cost of the course when deciding what to study.
- What other things did they consider to help them choose a course?

Other costs associated with further study

Books and other equipment

While course fees are the biggest cost of further study, they're not the only cost. You could also have to pay for books, materials, stationery or equipment. Exactly what you'll need and how much it'll cost will depend on what you're studying, but you could expect to have the following larger costs.

- **Textbooks**: These days, a lot of textbooks are available electronically, which has made them cheaper, or you could consider being a Savvy Saver and buying them second-hand to save money.
- **Laptop/computer:** You may also need a laptop (which you can take to uni with you) or a computer at home. These range in price, starting from around $300 to $400 up to several thousand dollars. To save money, you could always consider buying second-hand, but you'll need to make sure that it can run the latest versions of the software you'll need. Look out for sales, especially back to school sales at the beginning of the year, end of the financial year sales in June or the Cyber Monday sale in November. Some retailers also offer student discounts on study-related tech products, so ask about these, too.
- **Special equipment:** Depending on what you're studying you might also need some special equipment. For example, Mai needed a lab coat and safety glasses, which cost a total of $45,[22] while Bella had to pay $417 for a beauty therapist's uniform, robe, headband and mani/pedi kit.[23]

Student services and amenities fee

This fee is charged by further education providers to cover the cost of some of the on-campus services and facilities they provide. In 2022, the maximum student services and amenities fee a uni could charge was $315 per full-time student, per year. Some VET providers also charge a services and amenities fee, but there is no limit on how much this can be, so be sure to ask about this before you enrol.

Accommodation and living costs

You'll also need to consider whether you'll be able to continue living at home while you study, or if you want or need to move away.

Some unis have onsite accommodation for students, but if you study somewhere that doesn't have student accommodation, you'll need to rent a house or apartment, or move into a share house or apartment with other students. Besides paying rent, you'll probably also need to pay for utilities, such as gas, electricity, water and internet. And on top of that, food!

The costs of either onsite uni accommodation or a private rental will vary depending on where you move to. Generally, cities are more expensive to live in than regional areas. Most uni websites will have information about onsite accommodation, including the costs. You can compare these against the costs of private rentals (which you can find on real estate websites) or shared accommodation (which you can find on websites or social media groups).

Travel

If your course has on-campus classes, you might need to travel some distance to study, so you'll need to think about how you'll get there!

Perhaps you're like Bella, and bought a car during your gap year, or have access to one you can borrow. But if you're planning on driving, remember to factor in the cost of petrol, insurance, registration, maintenance and parking.

If you don't drive, or don't have a car, like Mai, look up the cost of public transport and the types available on your route.

Or, if the distances you have to travel aren't too great, and you're able to use a bicycle, you could consider cycling. Apart from the initial purchase cost, it's free to use and park. It's also good for the environment and will keep you fit!

How can I pay for these extra costs?

Work

If you didn't have a job while you were at high school, you'll probably need to get one to cover some of these costs. Most students easily combine work and study because, even if they're studying full-time, further education offers a more flexible timetable than school. You could even try to get a job in an industry related to your studies and gain some relevant work experience.

Government assistance

Depending on your circumstances, you might also qualify for government financial assistance when you're completing further study. This assistance is different from HECS-HELP/VSL/FEE-HELP. Some of these payments include:

- **Youth Allowance:** If you're between 18 and 24 and studying full-time, you may qualify depending on the value of your income and assets, or those of your parent or guardian.
- **Austudy:** You may qualify if you're over 25 and studying full-time, depending on the value of your income and assets.
- **ABSTUDY:** If you're of Aboriginal or Torres Strait Islander descent and studying full-time, there is a range of payments available to cover costs, including travel, course costs and living expenses.
- **Student Start-up Loan:** If you receive Youth Allowance, Austudy or ABSTUDY, you might qualify for a loan of $1,132 twice a year ($2,264 annually) to help cover some of your additional study costs. These loans are interest-free but are subject to indexation.
- **Rent Assistance:** If you receive Youth Allowance, Austudy or ABSTUDY and pay rent, you could be eligible for a rent assistance payment.
- **Tertiary Access Payment:** If you're moving from a regional/remote area to a metropolitan area for uni or a higher-level VET qualification, you could be eligible for a payment of up to $5,000 to help with the cost of moving, depending on how much your parent or guardian earns.
- **Relocation Scholarships:** If you receive ABSTUDY or Youth Allowance, and your studies require you to move from a regional/remote area to a metropolitan area to study, or the other way around, you could get a scholarship of up to $4,788 for each year of study at a uni or for a higher-level VET qualification.

For the most up-to-date information about government financial assistance, check the Services Australia website.

Taking a gap year

It's ok if you finish school and haven't got your next step planned out – there's heaps of time to figure it all out! Instead of going straight from school to uni or a VET course, some people (like Bella!) choose to take a gap year to work, save up, travel or just figure out what they want to do next. Taking some time away from studying can be a good breather after school, and it gives you a chance to think about what you want from your life.

After finishing school, Bella was lucky to find a full-time office job, where she worked for a year while she saved up and thought about her future plans. Although she enjoyed the work, she realised it was not her dream career and decided to enrol in her Diploma after her gap year was up. You might be like Bella, or you might find a job you fall in love with and want to stay there for a while. If that happens, by all means, see where it takes you, but always remember that you are in control of your journey.

If you're not sure what's next, but you know that you want to do something different, then further education is definitely something you should consider. As the first person in my family to graduate from uni, I can truly tell you that education can be life-changing. Because, Queens, knowledge is power, and gaining skills and qualifications really can help to secure your financial future.

ACTIVITY **How did the women in your life choose their careers?**

- Ask your mum, female guardian, aunt or older sister what they did after they finished high school.
- If they went on to further studies, or if they went straight into the workforce, why did they choose that path?

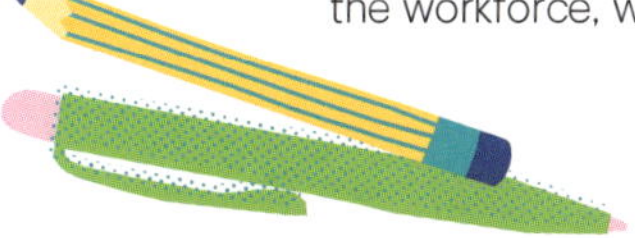

MONEY QUEENS TIP

REVISIT YOUR BUDGET

If you already set up a budget while you were in high school – well done! But now is the time to revisit that budget, because however you cover your costs after finishing high school, this is likely to be a time in your life when your expenses change dramatically. If you want to travel on a gap year, you'll need a plan to pay for that, and even if you still live at home, you might find your parents or guardians have new expectations about the things you should be paying for. For example, they might begin to charge you rent or expect you to contribute to some household expenses if they haven't previously. You'll also experience more freedom in the things you can do and places you can go when you turn 18, but these newfound freedoms can sometimes be expensive, so you'll need to tap into your inner Savvy Spender, Super Saver or even Stingy Squirrel to pay for them!

The good news is that this book has taught you all about budgeting, tracking your spending, and saving, and once you've got the hang these skills, they'll continue to be useful as you start doing more with your money.

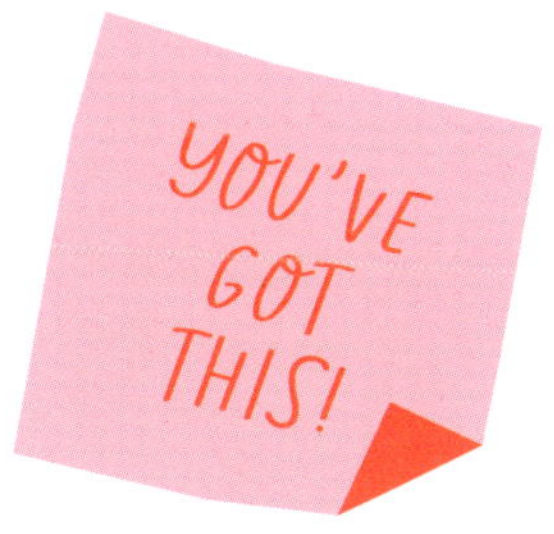

LOOKING AFTER FUTURE YOU

Hey, Queens, you know that feeling when you did something awesome yesterday that helps you today – like when you make your lunch for school the night before so you can hit snooze on your alarm for an extra 15 minutes the next morning? Yay, go yesterday you! Well, planning for your future is a little bit like that – it can seem like a hassle at the time, but if you make some smart decisions now, future you will be so happy.

Take retirement, for example. Right now it probably feels about 100 years away. But time has a way of sneaking up on you, and the cold, hard truth is that it's up to today you to look after future you – no one else is going to do it for you.

What do you think about when you hear the word 'retirement'? Bella imagines herself swanning around at social gatherings; Amina imagines travelling the world; Cam sees years of relaxation and trying new hobbies; and Mai pictures herself spoiling her grandkids. If you're imagining a fun, relaxing or exciting retirement like Amina, Bella, Mai and Cam, then it's going to take some money to achieve it. And the best thing you can do to make sure you have some money in retirement is to start taking care of your super while you're still young.

Super facts!

- Super – or superannuation – is a system of saving for retirement during your working years, and is one of the major sources of savings for retirement in Australia.
- If you're under 18, you need to earn more than $450 a month (before tax) **and** work more than 30 hours a week before your employer is required to put money into your super account, which is called the Super Guarantee. This might not happen most weeks or months, but could happen if you work extra shifts in the school holidays.
- Once you're over 18, your employer must pay you the Super Guarantee.
- The amount of money you receive under the Super Guarantee is based on how much you earn. It's currently 10.5% of your income but in the coming years it's scheduled to increase by 0.5% on 1 July each year until it reaches 12% in 2025.
- Your super money is invested, and usually can't be accessed until you're in your 60s.
- The money made on the super you have invested is reinvested, which helps your super grow even faster. This is called compounding and it's most effective when your money is invested for a long period of time.
- You can add to the payments made by your employer and put your own money into your super account to boost your retirement savings.
- Perhaps most importantly, as a woman you need to remember that you're likely to retire with less super than a man, largely due to factors that stem from the gender pay gap.

I can understand why Bella is confused! Bella's grandma gets the Age Pension, which is a payment the government makes to people with less money of their own to help them cover their living costs in retirement. But if Bella wants the kind of lavish retirement lifestyle she's dreaming of, she should be aware that the Age Pension doesn't provide enough money to enjoy a high standard of living – it just covers the essentials. That's why Bella's grandma can only afford to visit from interstate once a year. So, for Bella to fulfil her retirement dreams, she'll need some of her own money to help fund them. As with many things in life, money can't buy you happiness, but it can give you more choices. It truly is the *key that will unlock your dreams.*

Setting up your super

When you get your first job, it's possible your employer might ask for your super account details in case they have to pay you super. If you don't provide these details, they'll check with the Australian Taxation Office to see if you already have a super account. If you do, that's where they'll pay your super. And if you don't, your employer will automatically open an account for you with their default super fund. This is sometimes called a 'MySuper' account. This is typically a basic, low-fee account and your money will usually be invested in a balanced investment option. This account is ok, but to have more control over your super you may be better off choosing and opening your own super account.

Choosing a super fund

There are many different super funds you can open an account with. Some super funds may not allow people aged under 18 to open an account, or you may need a parent or guardian's help to open one. Some are specifically designed for younger people, while there are also super funds just for women or for self-employed workers.

Queens, like most things in the world of money, knowledge is power, and it pays to shop around! When doing this, there are a few important things to consider.

Fees	Most super funds charge fees, including account-keeping fees and investment fees. Fees are deducted from your super balance, so they can really eat into your money, especially when you're young and your super balance is low. So, look for an account that charges low or no fees and make sure you're not being charged for extras you don't need.
Investment options	You can choose how the money in your super account is invested, but different super funds offer different investment options. The choices available to you are usually based on how much risk you're willing to take in order to earn a higher return on your money. Typical options include conservative, balanced, growth and high growth. More and more funds also offer ethical or 'green' investment options.
Investment performance	Your super is invested with the aim of growing it, so you'll want to make sure the super fund you choose is good at investing money, too. You can compare the investment performance of different funds by using a financial comparison website, but make sure you look at the performance over at least five years and that you're comparing the same types of investment options against each other.

MONEY QUEENS TIP

YOU'RE NOT LOCKED IN FOR LIFE

Once you've chosen a super fund, remember that you're not locked into that fund forever. You can open a new account with a different super fund at any time if you feel it might be better for your circumstances and your money. But if you do this, be sure to transfer the super money from your old account into your new account and close your old account.

Growing your super

Getting a super account is the first step. Now, you need to make sure you're keeping an eye on the money being put in there from your employer, as well as how your fees and investment performance are affecting your super balance.

But there are other things that you can do to make your super grow, like putting your own money into it (called personal or voluntary contributions). There are some limits on the amount of money you can put into your super account each year, but these are in the tens of thousands of dollars, so it's unlikely to be a problem when you're young.

If you do decide to put some money into your super, and if you're under 18 and you've earned money from an employer (whether or not they've put any money into your super), you can claim a tax deduction for the personal contributions you've made. You can do this when you submit your tax return at the end of the financial year, which could reduce the amount of tax you have to pay. If you want to do this, you'll need to let your super fund know, and fill in a form, before you complete your tax return.

MONEY QUEENS TIP

PROVIDE YOUR TAX FILE NUMBER TO YOUR SUPER FUND

While it's not compulsory, it's really important to share your tax file number with your super fund. If you don't, they might not be able to accept any personal super contributions from you, or you might have to pay additional tax on the money put into your super account by your employer. Plus, you won't be able to benefit from government contributions into your super or claim a tax deduction on any contributions you make.

The government can also help you grow your super. If you're a low-income earner, put some of your own money into your super, and don't claim a tax deduction on it, you'll likely be eligible for something called a government co-contribution. This means for every dollar you put into your super, the government will contribute 50 cents, up to a limit of $500 a year. You don't need to apply to receive this money, but you do need to submit a tax return.

Similarly, you could also be eligible for another government super contribution called the low-income super tax offset, or LISTO. To qualify, you'll need to receive a payment from your employer into your super account. The amount of money you'll get from the government will be 15% of the amount that your employer has put into your super, up to a maximum of $500 a year. You don't need to apply or submit a tax return to be eligible for the LISTO payment, but your super fund needs to have your tax file number to process it.

I DON'T GET PAID SUPER BY MY EMPLOYER. SHOULD I OPEN A SUPER ACCOUNT ANYWAY?

If your employer isn't required to pay you super yet, you might be wondering, like Amina is, if you should open an account, and start putting some of your own money into your super – especially after everything I've told you about looking after future you! There can be some advantages to doing this, such as getting a tax deduction or having extra money added to it by the government. However, it's likely that you're not earning a huge amount of money, so you'll need to decide whether you'd rather just save any spare money instead.

How super works when you're self-employed or a contractor

Not everyone wants to work for someone else. If you're an aspiring entrepreneur, like Amina, or if you find work as a contractor or a freelancer rather than as an employee, it will be your responsibility to pay yourself super and to make sure you have some money for your retirement.

At a minimum, you should try to put the same amount of money into your super as an employer would (which is 10.5% of your income now, rising to 12% by 1 July 2025). You'll have many other expenses competing for your money, and it might be hard to prioritise your super, so here's a tip: many people who are self-employed or contractors include in their prices or service fees enough money to cover their super contributions. That way, it's effectively the customers who use the services who pay their super. To avoid the temptation of thinking that this extra money belongs to today you, not future you, you could look for a super fund that allows you to automate payments directly into your super account from your bank account on a regular basis.

But to really look after future you, you could also try to top up your super with your own additional contributions. If you're self-employed or a contractor, all of your super contributions are considered personal contributions, so you should be able to claim a tax deduction on them.

MONEY QUEENS TIP

REMEMBER TO CHECK YOUR SUPER!

Some employers do the wrong thing and don't pay any – or the right amount – of super. Whether this is accidental or on purpose, it's against the law. So, it's important to check that your employer is actually paying your super into your account. You can do this by checking your payslips against your super account statement. Your payslip will show the amount of super you've 'earned' each pay. You should also know that your employer is only required to actually deposit this money into your super account every three months.

If you discover that your super isn't being paid correctly, ask your employer about it. If the situation isn't resolved after that, you can report unpaid or underpaid super to the Australian Taxation Office through their website. If it's found that your super has been underpaid, your employer will be required to pay the super they owe you plus interest, since you missed out on earning investment returns on that money in your super account.

Queens, remember super is your money. It's there to help pay for the lifestyle of future you and so it's important to rule it!

Stick to one super account

It might sound like having multiple super accounts is a good thing, right? More accounts equals more money? Nope, in fact, it's more likely to be the opposite. This is because you'll be paying fees on each account, which will eat into the total amount of super savings you have. And, as you know, as a woman, you'll need to hang onto every dollar you have in super to avoid the gender retirement gap.

If you already have multiple super accounts, you can bring all of your super together into just one account. This is also known as consolidating it. This will save you money on account fees, boosting the amount of money you have for retirement, and it'll also make your super easier to manage. To consolidate your super, you can contact the Australian Taxation Office, or if you have a MyGov account you can do it online yourself.

Lost super is another big problem – some people have so many super accounts that they lose track of some of their super money altogether. Believe it or not, there's more than $13 billion of lost and unclaimed super in Australia![24]

Multiple accounts and lost super became such big problems that in November 2021, the government introduced a change to try to help people keep track of their super money more easily in the future. This change means that now, the first super account you open will be permanently attached to you – something called super stapling (ouch!). So, every time you start a new job, if you don't give them details of your super account, your employer will search to see if you already have a super account and pay your super into that instead of opening a new account for you.

CASE STUDY

Bella's multiple super accounts

If you've been working for a while like Bella, you might already have a super account with more than one fund. Bella has one account from the hospitality job she had when she was still at high school. And when she worked full-time in an office during her gap year, she chose to have an account opened with that employer's default fund, where her super was paid all year. Bella doesn't have a lot of super in either account, but she's paying fees on both and she isn't sure how either are investing her money. After a little research into the fees she's paying, the investment options available and how each fund has performed, Bella chooses to bring it all together in the first fund she ever had and selects her investment option. When Bella finds a new part-time job in the beauty industry to help her earn some money and gain experience while she's studying for her Diploma of Beauty Therapy, she has the super from that job paid there as well.

How your super can help you buy your first home

If you're anything like Cam and you already have in mind that you'd like to save for a home deposit, you'll be interested to know that super can play a role in this, too. Thanks to a change introduced by the government in 2017, you can now use your super as a way of saving some money to put towards a deposit to buy your first home. Under the First Home Super Saver Scheme, you can apply to have some money *you've* put into your super (not the money put in by your employer), along with the investment returns you've earned on that money, refunded to you to put towards a first home deposit.

To be eligible, you need to be over 18 and have never bought a property in Australia. You also must plan to live in the home you buy – so you can't take money out of your super to buy an investment property. The maximum amount you can withdraw is $50,000, providing you've put that much in personal contributions in.

If you've managed to contribute to your super, this could be an effective way to boost your savings towards a home deposit. However, if you decide to use some of your super money to help with buying a home, you'll need to remember that it will have an impact on the amount of super that's left for your retirement. If you make extra contributions into your super with the aim of using them to help you buy a home, but then decide not to withdraw money under the First Home Super Saver Scheme, you won't be able to access this money until you retire.

MY STORY

THE REAL-LIFE CONSEQUENCES OF NOT TAKING AN INTEREST IN YOUR SUPER

I have first-hand experience of the consequences of not paying attention to your super. By the time I turned 21, I'd worked in four different part-time jobs. I'd been paid super at three of these, but I'd never taken any interest in it, made any contributions to it myself, or consolidated my super into one account. I'd been paying fees on multiple accounts for years and wouldn't have been able to tell you the balance of each account, let alone what investment option my money was in or how those investments were performing.

When I got my first full-time job, my employer opened yet another super account in my name. At this point, I consolidated my super into one account, made an active choice about my investment option and started to make personal contributions to my super. But then I went on maternity leave, which turned into a five-year career break. When I went back to work, I did so as a contractor for another few years, and during that time (in my late 20s and early 30s) I neither received nor made any super contributions at all. Because I didn't know much about super when I was young, I missed out on the advantages of compounding that I could have benefited from if I'd tried to build up my super in my 20s.

For the past few years I've been running my own business and paying myself the same super contributions as an employer would, as well as making additional contributions. But it's fair to say that I'm a victim of both my own ignorance about super as a younger woman and the gender retirement gap, and my super balance is a lot lower than it should be. I'm desperately trying to catch up as my plan for retirement is to be boujee, not broke!

ACTIVITY **The women in your life and super**

- Ask your mum, female guardian or aunts about their own experiences with super.
- Are there things they wish they had done differently?

Tips for ruling your super

Queens, it's easy to think of super as boring, or a future problem, and to ignore it. One of the big reasons for this is because it doesn't seem like your money – it's separated from your pay, you never really see it and you can't benefit from it until you're much older. But it is yours – every single cent of it – and you should pay as much attention to it as you do the money in your bank account.

Here are seven tips to help you stay in charge and rule your super like a Queen.

1. As you change jobs, avoid opening multiple super accounts. And if you do have multiple accounts, decide which one best suits you at the moment and consolidate your super into one account.
2. If you can afford to, consider putting some (or more) of your own money into your super in the future.
3. Review how your super is invested from time to time to make sure you're still comfortable with the investment option it's in, and that it's appropriate for that point in your life. For example, a growth or high growth option might be better to help boost your super when you're young, while a conservative option could help protect the super you have as you approach retirement.
4. Keep an eye on your super but don't worry if the amount you have falls from time to time, unless you're really close to retirement. Investments do fall in value sometimes, but because super is a long-term investment, there should be time to recover any losses.

5. As you get older, you may have life insurance cover automatically added to your super. Be aware that the cost of this life insurance will be deducted from your super balance. You should also make sure the amount of life insurance you have is right for you. If you want to, you can always increase or decrease your life insurance or cancel it altogether.
6. Remember everything you've learned about the gender retirement gap and think about the impact that taking parental leave or working part-time will have on your super.
7. At any time, if you're not happy with your super fund's fees, performance, investment options or insurance cover, you can always open an account with another super fund and transfer your super across.

GROWING YOUR MONEY BY INVESTING

A money tree may be the stuff of fairytales, but just because you can't grow it out of the ground doesn't mean you can't grow your money at all, Queens. Investing is a way you can use some of your money to try to turn it into more money, and it's something to consider doing in the future, as you can't legally invest until you turn 18.

There are lots of different types of investments, such as shares, cryptocurrency, exchange traded funds and property. But even if you never invest in any of these, as soon as you have some super you become an investor, so it's worth learning about.

To help you rule your money, you'll need a bit of knowledge about what investing means and, if you're interested and able to give it a go one day, where to start. I also recommend doing some research of your own and asking advice from your parents or guardians as well as other family members or family friends.

Risk and return

Investing comes with a lot more risk than having your money sitting in the bank does. In fact, there's no guarantee your investments will increase in value at all – the value of investments goes up and down all the time, and they could even fall to the point where you lose all the money you invested!

So, why do people invest, if it's safer to leave their money sitting in a savings account? The answer is that investing can give you the opportunity to make more money (or a higher return) than you'd get from a savings account. Your money may be safer in the bank, but your interest rate (your return) may be low, so you don't have as much opportunity to grow your money.

When it comes to the terminology used in investing, low-risk investments (sometimes called conservative), have potential for low returns but smaller losses; medium-risk investments (sometimes called balanced), have potential for medium returns but also medium losses; and high-risk investments (sometimes called growth), have the potential for high returns but bigger losses. You'll also see these sorts of words used in relation to choosing the investment option for your super.

Your risk appetite

Different people feel differently about risk, which often comes back to their personality and life experiences. How much risk you're comfortable taking is sometimes called your risk appetite, and it's worth thinking about as it could affect your attitude to spending and saving, as well as investing.

In my experience, these are the four main risk appetites:

A CONSERVATIVE

B BALANCED

C MODERATE

D AGGRESSIVE

Quiz

To discover your risk appetite, take the risk quiz.

Q.1 Rain is forecast, but you're meant to be going to the beach with your friends. You:

- **A** Cancel straight away. The last thing you want is to be stuck at the beach in the rain.
- **B** Check some weather apps to find out more about the likelihood and timing of any rain before making a decision.
- **C** Go to the beach, but take an umbrella, just in case. Even with a bit of rain, it will still be fun!
- **D** Hope it's not going to rain, pack only your beach stuff and go – the weather forecast is always wrong, anyway!

Q.2 You're on a TV game show and can choose from one of the following prizes. Which would you choose?

- **A** $500 in cash.
- **B** A 50% chance of winning $3,000, plus $200 in cash.
- **C** A 25% chance of winning $10,000, plus $100 in cash.
- **D** A lottery ticket with a 1% chance of winning $1 million.

Q.3 You go to an amusement park with your family. You:

- **A** Have to be talked into riding the Ferris Wheel.
- **B** Watch a ride a few times before deciding whether it's for you.
- **C** Go on a few fast rides, but only if a friend will come with you.
- **D** Head straight for the highest, fastest, most upside-down rollercoaster in the park.

Q.4 Your cousin wants to start a dog-walking business, and asks you to invest $50 to help her set it up. When she's making a profit, she says she'll pay you back $60. You:

- **A** Say no. You're not sure the business will work, and she'll ever make the money to pay you back.
- **B** Ask her how much she's investing in it and only consider it if she's putting in more than you.
- **C** Say no to the $50 but offer to invest $30 and get $35 back once she's earned enough.
- **D** Give her the $50, no questions asked. Why not take a chance on your cousin?

Your risk appetite

MOSTLY A'S

CONSERVATIVE CAM

Like Cam, you're more of a glass-half-empty, worrier type. Before investing any money, you'd want to know the worst-case scenario as you think that's probably what will happen.

MOSTLY B'S

BALANCED BELLA

You're ok with a little bit of risk, but, like Bella, you do your research to weigh up the chances of both a positive and negative outcome before making decisions.

MOSTLY C'S

MODERATE MAI

Like Mai, you don't mind taking a risk, but you'll usually look for a way to minimise the risk you're taking and try to improve your chances of a positive outcome.

MOSTLY D'S

AGGRESSIVE AMINA

You love taking risks. In fact, the riskier the better is what Amina says! It may not always work out, but when it does it pays off and makes up for the times it doesn't.

Different types of investments

If you've heard of shares or cryptocurrency, then you've heard of a few types of investments. Some people might choose to invest their money in just one investment, while others might choose to 'diversify', or in other words, to spread their money between different investments rather than putting all their eggs in one basket. This can also help to reduce the risk they're taking if they use low-risk investments to balance out higher-risk ones.

But generally, Queens, the more money you've got to invest, the easier it will be to diversify your investments as you'll have more options for where you can invest it.

Shares

A share is a small piece of ownership of a company. Shares are bought and sold via a stock market. In Australia, the stock market is called the Australian Securities Exchange, or ASX for short. The price of an individual share in a company changes all the time and is determined by things such as:

- The number of shares a company is broken up into.
- How successful the company is.
- How many investors want to buy the shares.

There's a minimum amount you can invest in any company on the ASX, which is $500. There are lots of different companies to invest in, ranging from small to large, in all sorts of business sectors, from retail to healthcare, mining, or technology, just to name a few.

CASE STUDY:

How many shares $500 will buy

Exactly how many shares you'll get for $500 (or however much you've got to invest) will depend on the price of an individual share in the company you're interested in investing in. Let's take a look at how a $500 investment in imaginary companies Woy Technology and Zap Supermarkets will buy you a different number of shares in each.

	Woy Technology	Zap Supermarkets
Share price for one share at purchase	50 cents	$50.00
Number of shares for a $500 investment	1000 shares	10 shares

Shares in Zap Supermarkets are currently worth a lot more than shares in Woy Technology. There are a number of reasons why this could be the case: perhaps there are fewer shares available in Zap Supermarkets, which makes each one more valuable; or maybe they're having a lot of success, which means lots of investors want to buy their shares, pushing the price up.

Regardless of which of these companies you buy shares in, the value of your investment in the moment you make it is still $500. However, from that point on, the share price of each company could rise or fall at any time, changing the value of your investment.

There might also be a different amount of risk associated with investing in each of these companies. Woy Technology could become the next global tech giant with a share price to match if it creates a product that really takes off ... or it might go broke. By contrast, the share price of Zap Supermarkets is unlikely to double, but it's also unlikely to go out of business.

MONEY QUEENS TIP

BLUE-CHIP SHARES AND DIVIDENDS

Shares in Zap Supermarkets are what are known as blue-chip shares. These are the largest and most successful companies on the stock market. (The name, blue-chip, comes from poker, where the blue gambling chips are worth the most money.)

Blue-chip companies usually pay their shareholders (the people who own shares in the company) something called dividends, which is where they give a portion of the profits they make to their shareholders, usually a couple of times a year. This dividend money is paid in addition to any money you'd make if you sell the shares for more than you bought them for. While getting paid dividends isn't guaranteed, blue-chip shares are popular with people who are looking for a reliable return rather than a large increase in the share price.

The opposite of a blue-chip share is a penny share, named after the British term for cents due to their low share price. Investing in these shares is usually riskier and these companies don't pay dividends, either because they're not making any profits yet, or because they reinvest any money they make to grow the business.

Exchange traded funds

An exchange traded fund (ETF) is a type of investment you might choose instead of buying shares directly in one company.

An ETF is a fund that buys shares in different companies. So, instead of buying a share, which is a little piece of a company, you will buy a unit, which is a little piece of the fund. You do this via the stock market, in the same way as you would buy shares.

The benefit of buying units in an ETF is that each unit gives you a tiny piece of ownership in all of the shares the fund owns. If you don't have much money to invest, your investment will be more diversified than if you bought shares directly in just one or two companies.

There are more than 200 ETFs trading on the ASX, all with different investment strategies. Some invest in a mix of the largest companies on the ASX, while others focus on small or mid-sized companies. Some invest in global companies that trade on other stock markets around the world, while others focus on investing in companies in one business sector, such as technology.

Like shares, the minimum investment in an ETF is $500, and just like shares, the price of ETF units can go up and down. The companies who create and manage ETFs also charge a fee, which is incorporated in the unit price of the ETF.

The cheapest and easiest way to buy and sell shares or units in an ETF is online. When you buy or sell either shares or ETF units, you pay a transaction fee charged by the share trading business. This is called brokerage. All the big banks have online share-trading businesses, but there are lots of others around, too, and they usually have cheaper brokerage. You should be able to find an online share trader that charges around $10 for brokerage, and you'll need to pay this amount on top of the money you invest.

Micro-investing

Micro-investing is a fairly new type of app-based investing. You need to be at least 18 to sign up for an account with a micro-investing app and can start investing by depositing money (usually a minimum of $50 to $100) into your app investment account. Some of these apps also offer a round-up feature, where you can choose to round up your everyday spending to the nearest dollar and the difference is deposited into your investment account.

You choose an investment option and the app pools the money deposited by individual investors until it has enough to buy units in an ETF or company shares. As an investor, you essentially own part of an ETF unit, or part of a share, with the amount you own determined by the amount you invested. This is called fractional investment. In return for access to the app, you're charged brokerage or an account management fee.

Property

Not all types of investing are done through the stock market. Property is another thing that people invest in to grow their money. Some people buy an investment property, which they don't live in but rent out to others. This provides them with regular money in the form of the rent they receive, and if the property increases in value, they can also sell it for a profit. But buying a property is very expensive, so it's unlikely to be something you'd be able to afford to invest in when you're young.

I'VE HEARD ABOUT CRYPTOCURRENCY, BUT I DON'T REALLY UNDERSTAND IT. CAN I INVEST IN IT?

I'm sure that you, like Bella, have heard the word 'cryptocurrency' – or 'crypto'. If you have, you might not be sure what it is. Cryptocurrencies are a digital form of payment that can be used to buy things as an alternative to traditional dollars and cents. The most well known cryptocurrency is Bitcoin, although there are lots of others.

Cryptocurrencies are also becoming increasingly popular as investments – they can be bought as an investment in the hope that they will increase in value and can then be sold for a profit. But beware: cryptocurrencies are a high-risk investment. The price of Bitcoin, for example has ranged from less than US 0.01 cent per coin to as high as US$68,000 per coin, but it has experienced a lot of big falls and rises in between that have both lost and made money for investors. While there are some great get-rich-quick stories around about the earliest investors in cryptocurrencies, the potential to make a lot of money by being an early investor has probably already passed.

So, if Bella chooses to invest in something as high-risk as cryptocurrency, she'll need to accept that she might lose all the money she invests. If she does decide to go ahead, it's possible to invest in cryptocurrency both directly, by buying individual cryptocurrencies, and indirectly, through an ETF, or a micro-investing app.

But, Queens, perhaps the most important part of Bella's question is where she says she doesn't really understand cryptocurrency. It's never a good idea to invest in something you don't understand. If Bella's really keen on buying cryptocurrencies, she should spend some time learning a lot more about them before doing so.

It's very unlikely that Mai's investments will increase in value significantly overnight, so she will need to be patient when it comes to investing. Mai should also know that she's likely to see the value of her investments fall as well as rise, which is known as volatility.

Before she starts, it will help if Mai has a clear goal behind why she's investing, or an outcome she wants to achieve (such as to grow her money to the point where she has enough for a home deposit). This will guide her when making decisions about when to sell her investments, or whether to be worried if they fall in value from time to time.

Reacting emotionally and panic-selling when her investments fall in value could be one of the worst things Mai does, especially if she's planned to invest for the long-term. This is because history tells us that if she takes a long term approach, Mai's more likely to make money than to lose it by investing in the stock market.

How time and patience can help grow your money[25]

$10,000
invested in 1990

$177,299
value by 2020*

8.55%
average return per year

*Invested in Australia's 200 largest companies, no investments sold and all dividends reinvested.

Interested in investing? Do your homework first!

Queens, remember that knowledge is power, so before you decide to make any investment, you should do plenty of research.

In the case of shares, checking out the company's website can help you understand what it does, and when researching an ETF or micro-investing app, you'll need to find out the types of companies or sectors it invests in, so you can research those. Likewise, you should research any cryptocurrencies you might be interested in investing in, as well as the whole alternative payment market in general. And with property, you'll need to know about growth suburbs, different property types and rental returns in different locations.

In all cases, reading business websites or the business section of newspapers can help you understand what's happening in the world of business. All investments can be positively or negatively affected by what's going on in the world, so it helps to know how your potential investments could fare as a result of things happening in the news.

Ultimately, you're performing research to ensure that you don't lose the $500 (or more) that you're considering investing, or that you've already invested. After all, the reason you're investing is to grow your money, which won't happen if you sell your shares, ETF units, micro-investments, cryptocurrency or property below what you bought them for!

ACTIVITY **Does anyone in your family invest?**

- Ask your parent, guardian, grandparent, aunt or uncle about their experiences with investing.
- If they do invest, ask them about the types of investments they have and how they go about researching them.
- If they don't invest, ask them if they've ever considered it.

Values-based investing

Queens, I know that you all have issues that are important to you and changes that you want to see in the world. Maybe you're like Mai, and feel passionate about animal rights. Perhaps you avoid buying fast fashion, like Cam, or advocate for better social equality, like Bella, or attend climate rallies, like Amina.

Whatever it is that you're passionate about (and maybe it's all of the above!) – by now you know that you can choose to spend and use your money to support the things you care about, and to avoid supporting the things you don't. It's the same with investing, too. Many people make investment choices that align with their personal values.

For example, Amina could choose to avoid buying shares in companies involved in the production of fossil fuels; Cam could buy shares in sustainable and ethical fashion companies; and Amina and Mai might be interested in ETFs that invest in companies trying to bring about positive change, like solar or wind farm businesses, medical companies or education providers.

As with all investing, remember to perform lots of research and ask for advice from people you trust before you make a decision about values-based investing.

MONEY QUEENS TIP

CHARITY DONATIONS

We've spoken a lot about using your money to support the things you care about, whether that's choosing a bank or super account that makes ethical investments, or spending money or investing in companies that want to do good things in the world. But another way you can use your money to do good is by supporting charities or causes that you care about. You will feel a great sense of satisfaction and pride in donating to a charity that means a lot to you or helping a friend or family member out by sponsoring them in a fun run. It's also worth knowing that charitable donations are tax-deductible, so not only are you contributing to a cause that's important to you, you're also potentially reducing the amount of tax you have to pay.

If you don't have enough money to invest yet, or you're conservative about risk like Cam, you could consider getting some investing practice by using hypothetical money, pretending you've invested it and watching to see what happens. You could also do this alongside a parent, guardian or other trusted adult and they can teach you what they know about investing, or you can learn together.

ACTIVITY **Practise investing without the investments**

Imagine you have $10,000 to invest.

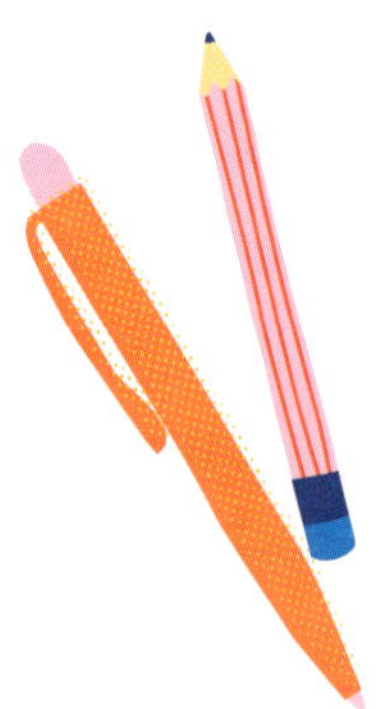

- Research some companies or ETFs and read some business news articles online or in the paper, like I told you about earlier. Take your time with this research as it's going to be very important in helping you decide which companies or ETFs you'd invest in.
- Once you've picked your investments, decide how much money you'd invest in each ETF or company.
- Regularly keep track of the 'closing price' of the shares or units you're 'invested' in, which are published at the end of each day on the ASX website. It also helps to keep up with business news to try to work out why the prices went up or down. Keep a note of these movements and any research that you've found.
- At the end of three months, work out the value of your investments based on the current share price and calculate whether you made or lost money. Then, do the same for the next three months and see what changes.
- This imaginary investment tracker will be a great way to show you the research and patience that's required for investing, and give you a real idea about whether you're interested in and confident about making investment decisions.

Women and investing – another gender gap!

By now you'll be aware of (and probably very angry about) the gap between men and women when it comes to money. This is the case for investing, too: currently, more men than women invest in the stock market in Australia, with women making up just 18% of all investors.[26] Research also shows that women have fewer investments than men, that the value of our investments is lower, that our investments are less diversified, and that we're more conservative than men when it comes to taking investment risks.

But here's where it gets interesting ... studies have found that women are actually better at investing than men![27] We spend more time researching our investments; we're better at matching them to our goals in life; and we remain calm when prices rise or fall, which means we buy and sell our investments less often than men.

Some of the major barriers preventing more women from investing include a lack of money to invest and a lack of knowledge and confidence about investing. Queens, I hope that what you've learned in this book might help with the money side of things and that I've given you a little more knowledge about investing. So, when you're ruling your money later in life, you might feel confident enough to give investing a go, if it feels right for you.

THE END… OR JUST THE BEGINNING?

Queens, you may have reached the end of this book, but this is just the beginning of your lifelong journey with money. As I leave you here, I'd like to send you off with three final messages.

1. **Doing is better than perfect, so just start!**

   I've never forgotten these words of wisdom from a wise Queen. I hope you feel like you've got the knowledge you need to start ruling your money, so you can live the life of your dreams, whatever that may be. But even if you still feel a bit uncertain, the best thing you can do is to just start anyway! If you feel like you don't know everything there is to know, then that's a feeling you'll need to get used to. The reality is that with money, as with all things in life, there will always be more to learn along the way. And if you wait until you feel sure you'll be able to do things perfectly, there's a good chance that day may never come.

2. **Money can't buy happiness, but it can buy choices and security.**

   While money doesn't necessarily hold the key to happiness, it can give you a lot more choices in life. I truly believe the mantra that I shared with you at the start of this book – that money is the key that will unlock your dreams. In my case, it's certainly proven to be true. I wasn't born rich, but thanks to the journey I've been on, learning about, understanding and finally mastering my money, I've gone from broke to boujee. And if I can do it, you can, too.

3. **Big things often start small.**

   Queens, you'll now know that all's not equal between men and women in the world of money, and the truth is that some big changes at a society level are needed to change the situation. But also, don't underestimate the impact that each and every one of you can have on driving those changes. If enough Queens demand financial equality from future partners, employers and politicians, the pressure for these bigger changes will build until it can no longer be ignored.

So, Queens, let's go! It's time to flip the script and take control of our financial futures – just like men have been doing forever. Because the *sooner* you start taking care of your money, the *faster* it will be able to start taking care of you and the *easier* it will be to overcome these gender disadvantages. You've got this, Queens!

RESOURCES

Things will constantly change in your lives, and what's important or relevant to you right now might not be the same when you're in your 20s or 30s and onwards. But having a good foundation with money – like knowing how to budget, how to track your spending, and how to save – are skills that you can take with you through life. I hope you'll be able to come back to this book many times over the coming years to help you with this!

But there are lots of other resources you can use to learn more about ruling your money, too. I've listed some that you can turn to for more information on some of the topics discussed in the book. Keep in mind that things are constantly changing in the world of money, so it's a good idea to stay up-to-date with changes to things that may affect your money journey, like tax, HELP loan repayments, credit card and buy now pay later terms and conditions, and government financial assistance.

Up-to-date, general money information:
www.moneysmart.gov.au

Tax and super information:
www.ato.gov.au

Information about work and pay entitlements:
www.fairwork.gov.au

More on the gender pay gap:
www.wgea.gov.au

Government financial assistance:
www.servicesaustralia.gov.au

Information on money and relationships:
www.womentalkmoney.org.au

Help with financial abuse:
www.financialcounsellingaustralia.org.au
www.kidshelpline.com.au
www.whiteribbon.org.au

Credit and debt help:
www.ndh.org.au

Information on further education debt:
www.studyassist.gov.au

Help to find a uni degree:
www.uac.edu.au

Help to find a VET course:
www.myskills.gov.au

To check your further education loan balance:
www.myhelpbalance.gov.au

More on investing in shares or ETFs in Australia:
www.asx.com.au/investors/start-investing

Consumer complaints about financial products:
www.afca.org.au

Agencies you can access your credit report from:
www.experian.com.au/order-credit-report
www.creditcheck.illion.com.au
www.equifax.com.au/personal/products/credit-and-identity-products

Financial comparison websites:
www.finder.com.au
www.canstar.com.au
www.ratecity.com.au
www.mozo.com.au

Job search websites:
www.seek.com.au
www.careerone.com.au

You can also visit the Money Queens website, www.moneyqueens.com.au, for downloadable resources, articles and up-to-date information about how to rule your money, or follow me on Instagram @money.queens.au.

GLOSSARY

After-tax income: the money you earn after tax has been taken out of your income.

ATM: Automatic Teller Machine, the machines that you can use to withdraw money from the bank.

Australian Securities Exchange: the share market in Australia, also known as the ASX.

Balance: the total amount of money you have or debt you owe.

Before-tax income: the money you earn before tax has been taken out of your income.

Brokerage: the transaction fee you pay when you buy or sell assets (such as shares).

Budget: a plan for your money which lists the amount of money you have coming in (income) and the amount of money you have going out (expenses).

Buy now pay later: a form of credit that enables you to pay for an item or service, use it immediately and pay back the cost of the item or service in regular installments over time. Sometimes called BNPL.

Census date: the date when your enrolment in a unit of study at university is finalised and you become liable to pay for it.

Commonwealth supported place: a government-subsidised place at university, which means the government pays for some of the cost of your uni degree. Also called a CSP.

Compounding: when the income made from investing is reinvested to increase your overall investment.

Compulsory repayment threshold: the amount of income you have to be receiving to start paying back your higher education loans.

Credit: money loaned by a bank or other financial services provider under an agreement that it will be paid back.

Credit card: a card that enables you to spend money you don't have or to withdraw money you don't have from an ATM.

Credit limit: the maximum amount you can spend on your credit card.

Credit rating: a score calculated based on your history using credit, which lenders use to assess how likely you are to repay debts when deciding whether to lend you money.

Cryptocurrency: a digital form of money that can be used when buying and selling things and is also bought and sold as an asset.

Curriculum vitae (or CV): a document that lists your contact details and any skills or experience you might have that are relevant to getting a job. Also called a résumé.

Debit card: a card that can be used to pay for things with money from your bank account or to withdraw money from your bank account at an ATM.

Debt: money you owe, either to a person, business or the government.

Diversification: spreading your risk between different investments in order to reduce your overall risk.

Dividend: a portion of the profits made by a company that is paid to its shareholders.

Emergency fund: a savings bank account set aside for use in emergency situations, such as to pay for unexpected expenses.

Equal pay: people with the same experience and qualifications being paid the same amount. Not paying people equally in these circumstances is illegal in Australia.

Exchange traded fund: an investment fund listed on a stock market that buys assets (such as shares) and sells units of its fund to investors, giving them a small piece of ownership of its assets. Also known as ETFs.

Expenses: things you have to spend money on.

FEE-HELP: Full Fee-Higher Education Loan Program. This is the program the government uses to loan full-fee paying Australian citizens the money to pay for university and vocational education and training.

Financial abuse: when someone you're in a relationship with is stopping you from accessing your money, negatively influencing your decisions about money or using your money without your consent.

Financial year: a year that starts on 1 July and ends on 30 June the next calendar year.

Gender pay gap: the difference in average earnings from full-time work between men and women.

Gender retirement gap: the difference in the average amount of superannuation savings between men and women at retirement.

Good debt: debt that has the potential to increase your wealth.

Hardship assistance: help offered by banks and other financial services and utilities providers if you're having trouble paying bills or loans.

HECS-HELP: stands for Higher Education Contribution Scheme-Higher Education Loan Program. This is the program the government uses to loan Australian citizens the money to pay for university.

HELP loan limit: the total amount you can borrow under the government's further education loan program over your lifetime.

Income: money you receive, from work or investments.

Indexation: an adjustment made to

the value of investments or loans based on inflation.

Inflation: increases in the cost of living in society.

Interest: money you receive when you lend your money to someone (or a bank) or money that you pay when you borrow money.

Interest rate: the amount of money you will receive when you loan money or pay when you borrow money, usually expressed as a percentage.

Investing: when money is used to buy assets with the expectation that these will increase in value.

Investment option: the choice you have for how the money in your superannuation account is invested.

Lay-by: a system of paying for an item in instalments where you only receive the item when the final instalment has been paid.

Micro-investing: ownership of a small part of an asset (such as a share or ETF unit). Also called fractional investment.

Minimum monthly repayment: the minimum amount you have to pay off a credit card each month.

Parental leave: a form of leave from work offered when people have a baby or adopt a child.

Payslip: a record that shows details of your pay during a pay period, including the hours you've worked, your rate of pay per hour, the total amount you've earned before tax, the total amount you've earned after tax and the amount of super your employer was required to pay (if any) during that pay period.

Personal contribution: money that you choose to add to your superannuation, beyond the super paid by your employer. Also called a voluntary contribution.

Return: money you make from investing or saving your money.

Risk appetite: how comfortable or willing you are to take risks.

Savings account: a type of bank account used for saving money.

Share: a small piece of ownership in a company. Sometimes called a stock.

Statement: a summary of transactions that have occurred during a set period of time. Banks and super funds issue statements.

Stock market: the place where shares are bought and sold. In Australia, it is called the Australian Securities Exchange (or ASX).

Student contribution: the remaining amount you have to pay towards your uni degree if you have a CSP. You can use the HECS-HELP system to pay for this.

Subsidised place: a government subsidised place at a VET provider, which means the government pays for some of the cost of your VET qualification.

Super account: an account with a super fund that your superannuation money is put into.

Superannuation (or super): a compulsory system of saving for retirement during your working years.

Super Guarantee: the percentage of your earnings your employer is legally required to put into your superannuation. Sometimes called SG.

Surcharge: an additional charge or fee that is added to the cost of something. It is often charged when you use a credit card to pay for something.

Taxation: money collected by the government from workers to pay for essential services in society, such as schools, hospitals and roads. Also called tax.

Tax File Number: a unique number that is used to identify you in the tax system.

Tax deduction: expenses or costs that you can claim to help reduce the amount of tax you have to pay.

Tax return: a summary of money earned, tax paid and tax deductions, which workers are required to submit to the government at the end of every financial year.

Transaction account: a type of bank account used for everyday banking, such as having income paid into or paying for expenses out of.

VET: stands for Vocational Education and Training, an alternative option to university for further study beyond high school.

Volatility: the frequency of movements in the price of an asset (such as shares), either up or down.

VSL: stands for VET Student Loan. This is part of HELP, which the government uses to loan Australian citizens the money to pay for vocational education and training.

SOURCES

1 & 2 https://www.wgea.gov.au/publications/australias-gender-pay-gap-statistics

3 https://www.wgea.gov.au/publications/gender-segregation-in-australias-workforce, table 5.

4 & 5 https://www.wgea.gov.au/sites/default/files/documents/australian-unpaid-care-work-and-the-labour-market.pdf, table 1.

6 https://www.abs.gov.au/statistics/labour/employment-and-unemployment/labour-force-australia/latest-release#key-statistics, table 1.

7 https://www.abs.gov.au/statistics/people/people-and-communities/gender-indicators-australia/latest-release#work-and-family-balance

8 & 9 https://www.superannuation.asn.au/ArticleDocuments/270/2022_Superannuation_Account_Balances_Research.pdf.aspx?Embed=Y

10 https://www.smh.com.au/money/super-and-retirement/entrenched-gender-divide-in-voluntary-super-contributions-20200720-p55dqf.html

11 https://www.corelogic.com.au/women-and-property

12 https://onlinelibrary.wiley.com/doi/full/10.1111/1753-6405.12651

13 https://rlc.org.au/sites/default/files/attachments/UNSW%20report%201%20-%20Financial%20Abuse%20and%20IPV%20-%20PDF%20version%20-%20Final.pdf

14 https://asic.gov.au/media/5852803/rep672-published-16-november-2020-2.pdf

15 https://asic.gov.au/about-asic/news-centre/find-a-media-release/2018-releases/18-201mr-asic-s-review-of-credit-cards-reveals-more-than-one-in-six-consumers-struggling-with-credit-card-debt/

16 & 17 https://asic.gov.au/media/5852803/rep672-published-16-november-2020-2.pdf

18 https://www.dese.gov.au/higher-education-loan-program/resources/2022-allocation-units-study-funding-clusters

19 https://www.nationalskillscommission.gov.au/insights/vet-fees-subsidies-and-prices-across-australia

20 https://au.talent.com/salary?job=graduate+engineer

21 https://au.talent.com/salary?job=beauty+therapist

22 https://engineering.sydneyestore.com.au/

23 https://cmatraining.app.box.com/s/s52na6h9zknkzuhgr518ehudey1bi8zv

24 https://www.ato.gov.au/about-ato/research-and-statistics/in-detail/super-statistics/super-accounts-data/lost-and-unclaimed-super-by-postcode/

25 https://www.fidelity.com.au/insights/resources/adviser-resources/sharemarket-chart/a4-handout/

26 https://www.investors.asn.au/magazine/why-do-so-few-women-invest/

27 https://www.businessthink.unsw.edu.au/articles/women-trading-investment-investors

'I AM SICK OF CRAWLING TOWARD A WORLD OF GENDER EQUALITY. IT'S TIME TO RUN.'

– JULIA GILLARD

ACKNOWLEDGEMENTS

They say it takes a village and perhaps the most important lesson I've learned in my life is that women do best when we lift each other up, rather than competing with each other. Girls – other women are not the competition. So, it seems fitting that the skills, talents and time of so many amazing girls and women have contributed to the making of this book and I am beyond grateful to each and every one of them.

I first came up with the idea for this book in response to the frustration I felt in early 2021 when women's issues were dominating politics and the news. I felt a deep dismay at how little progress my generation of women had made in the push for equality. I looked at where my skills and expertise lay and for something meaningful I could do to contribute to the cause of helping my daughters and all of tomorrow's women and this was my answer.

In particular, I am indebted to Simone Redman-Jones, a wonderful cheerleader of women who I've known since the age of 12. She was the first person I ran my idea by and it was her resounding 'hell yes' that gave me the courage to have a go. Simone's undying enthusiasm, pep talks and belief in me when my own self-belief wavered have been the wind in my sails throughout this process, and her marketing nous hasn't hurt, either.

To my publisher, Tash Besliev – you understood what I was trying to achieve from our first conversation and also said 'hell yes', backing both me and this book from the outset. Thank you. To my editor, Coral Huckstep – this book has been a beast and even though it took some wrangling I know you agree it's important work. Every suggestion, change, question and comment from you made it better. My gratitude also extends to Freya Horton Andrews for the rigorous proofread, to Laura McNicol Smith and the publicity, sales and marketing department, and to the entire team at Affirm Press for backing books that make a difference. There was no other place this could have happened and this book undoubtedly found the right home.

The illustrator and designer of *Money Queens*, Kushla Ross, has taken what were words on a page and elevated them to the next level. I am so grateful for your talent and intuitive understanding of this project. It is hard to overstate the impact of good design and colour to bring life and energy and create engagement with a topic that can be dry at times.

To my first readers: my teenage daughters Holly Bowes and Daisy Bowes for being my in-house focus group, my friends and flat-out smart women Simone Redman-Jones, Julie May and Anna Foundling for their guidance, wisdom and sense checking, and to Christian Bowes, for ensuring my figures always stack up.

Special thanks also to Gerard Brody, CEO of the Consumer Action Law Centre for reviewing the chapter on credit and debt to ensure that it accurately reflected the types of situations his wonderful organisation unfortunately encounters on a daily basis, and to superannuation guru Fabian Bussoletti for his knowledge and guidance in reviewing the superannuation content.

To all the other fabulous Queens who have supported me with pep talks, endless encouragement or have generously given their time to help with *Money Queens* in one way or another, thank you all.

Finally, to Christian, Holly, Daisy and Harry, who gave me the time and space to try to help girls everywhere, even if they sometimes suffered in the process. My girls, you are the Queens of the future – do me proud. My boys, you are the best kind of men. And to my mum, Ann, who let me watch her budget and always encouraged me to follow my dreams.